The Brainstorms Family
Epilepsy On Our Terms

*Stories by Children with Seizures
and Their Parents*

COMMENTS ON
BRAINSTORMS: EPILEPSY IN OUR WORDS

This collection might help nonspecialists more accurately interpret medical histories of patients with atypical seizures. Certainly it tells us vividly what these patients experience. A novel and attractive approach to improving diagnostic interpretation.

Annals of Internal Medicine

... the essence of the book ... has fulfilled the author's intent to alleviate from those patients with seizures who have a sense of isolation the fear of feeling they are insane or crazy because of their weird experiences. It indicates that there are others having similar unusual experiences and they may even find a description of a seizure in here which is similar to their own.

Electroencephalography and Clinical Neurophysiology
Linda Moretti Ojeman
Dept. of Neurology
Regional Epilepsy Center
University of Washington
Seattle, WA

This small book is enlightening in many respects with its witty and touching descriptions. It brings to life our ambiguous medical terminology, and improves our understanding of the impact of this affliction on the quality of life ... I consider this book essential reading for anyone interested in this field.

Youssef G. Comair, M.D.
The Cleveland Clinic Foundation
Cleveland, Ohio

You cannot imagine how much it (the book) has helped me to accept epilepsy as something I'm just going to have to live with. Just knowing that I'm not the only one that has gone through some of these experiences makes it easier.

A Reader

This is an interesting and valuable little book in which Steven Schachter shares with us the experiences of his epilepsy patients in their own words. ... In no area of neurology is the history more important than in epilepsy, not only in making a correct diagnosis but in understanding the patient as a human being and partner in the therapeutic process.

Neurology

Dr. Schachter is to be congratulated on a useful and interesting book.

European Journal of Medicine

... the first book of its kind.

USA Today

This is a wonderful book. Dr. Schachter has done a great service to epilepsy patients and their doctors, particularly the former, in compiling this comprehensive collection of the experiences of those suffering this unique disorder . . . and in their own words. The seizure descriptions detail the rich fabric of human experience as reflected in the epileptic process . . . [they] attest to the often bizarre nature of epileptic symptoms, the pain inflicted, the loneliness of the experience, and the remarkable courage of these patients.

A. James Rowan, M.D.
Professor of Neurology
Mount Sinai School of Medicine
Chief, Neurology Service
Bronx DVA Medical Center

COMMENTS ON
THE BRAINSTORMS COMPANION:
EPILEPSY IN OUR VIEW

Books about epilepsy are not often emotional, nor do they usually elicit empathy. Indeed, they usually [only] cover the hard facts of the illness. This book is different. . . . These accounts of seizures remind us of the tremendous drama of witnessing them.

This is a very helpful book for patients, their relatives, and others who might witness seizures, as well as for the medical profession, especially those treating patients with epilepsy. It will enable us to deal better with the patient and the family and will no doubt increase our understanding into the emotional challenge of having epilepsy.

Elinor Ben-Menachem, Epilepsia

This book describes well the views and feelings of those who live with persons with epilepsy. It will enable physicians, care-givers, and educators . . . to better understand and to respond appropriately [to seizures]. . . . This is an excellent book of descriptions and views, and provides invaluable advice for physicians, care-givers, and paramedics.

Th. de Barsy, Extrait De La Revue Des Questions Scientifiques

I would recommend that all patients with epilepsy own a copy of this book. It should also be included in medical bookstores and medical and community libraries.

Tonya F. Fuller, Doody's Health Sciences Book Review Journal

By reading this book, neurologists and paramedics will gain a greater awareness of the emotions and sensitivities of patients with epilepsy and those who surround them.

Andrea Bernasconi, European Neurology

THE BRAINSTORMS FAMILY
EPILEPSY ON OUR TERMS

*Stories by Children with Seizures
and Their Parents*

Steven C. Schachter, M.D.
*Comprehensive Epilepsy Center
Beth Israel Hospital;
Harvard Medical School
Boston, Massachusetts*

Georgia D. Montouris, M.D.
*Epi-Care Center
Semmes-Murphey Clinic;
University of Tennessee
Memphis, Tennessee*

John M. Pellock, M.D.
*Comprehensive Epilepsy Clinics
MCV Hospitals;
Medical College of Virginia
Virginia Commonwealth
University
Richmond, Virginia*

Lippincott - Raven
P U B L I S H E R S
Philadelphia • New York

Printed in the United States of America.

Schachter, Steven C.
  The brainstorms family : epilepsy on our terms : stories by children with seizures and their parents / Steven C. Schachter, Georgia D. Montouris, John M. Pellock.
      p.   cm.
  Includes bibliographical references and index.
  Summary: Presents information about the condition of epilepsy, what it is like to have seizures, the different kinds of seizures, and the effects of epilepsy on the individual and the family.
    ISBN 0-397-51839-0
    1. Epilepsy in children—Juvenile literature.   2. Epilepsy in children—Popular works. [1. Epilepsy.   2. Diseases.]
  I. Montouris, Georgia D.   II. Pellock, John M.   III. Title.
RJ496.E6S32   1996
618.92'853—dc21   96-45080
                                                                          CIP

Care has been taken to confirm the accuracy of the information presented and to describe generally accepted practices. However, the authors, editors, and publisher are not responsible for errors or omissions or for any consequences from application of the information in this book and make no warranty, express or implied, with respect to the contents of the publication.

The authors, editors, and publisher have exerted every effort to ensure that drug selection and dosage set forth in this text are in accordance with current recommendations and practice at the time of publication. However, in view of ongoing research, changes in government regulations, and the constant flow of information relating to drug therapy and drug reactions, the reader is urged to check the package insert for each drug for any change in indications and dosage and for added warnings and precautions. This is particularly important when the recommended agent is a new or infrequently employed drug.

Some drugs and medical devices presented in this publication have Food and Drug Administration (FDA) clearance for limited use in restricted research settings. It is the responsibility of the health care provider to ascertain the FDA status of each drug or device planned for use in their clinical practice.

9   8   7   6   5   4   3   2   1

Art on the front and back covers is by Jacqui Streeton.

Dedication

This book is dedicated to all children with epilepsy and their families.

CONTENTS

Jaime Lyn Bauer

FOREWORD

I wish with all my being that I could turn the clock back to when the enemy, epilepsy, came into our lives, not so that I could experience the sometimes overwhelming emotions a thousand times more but so that I could avoid and therefore erase the many mistakes that we made because of our ignorance. Reading *The Brainstorms Family: Epilepsy on Our Terms* was very painful for me. I could not keep myself from weeping. I understood all too well what the parents and children quoted in this book had experienced, and yet I felt compelled to read on because I could identify with all of them. I was not a bad parent, I was not an idiot, I was not alone. . . . I wish I had known earlier. Having had access to this book all those years ago would have made immeasurable differences. It is in knowing what this book can do for you that I share some of our experiences along with the knowledge I wish I'd had.

We have been living with epilepsy for nine and a half years. My husband's response to our son's first seizure was only the beginning of a dynamic process that is too often the norm. One parent, usually the father, is in denial. *Denial* brings about *isolation* of the other parent and the child with epilepsy. That child is often *rejected* and *blamed* by the parent in denial, in an attempt by the parent to distance himself or herself from the problem. This places tremendous pressure on the marriage relationship and, ultimately, on the entire family. Denial encourages a commitment (sometimes unspoken) to conceal the illness at all costs, resulting in shame. It evokes anger in each family member, which is ultimately directed at the person who needs it the least: the child experiencing the terrifying effects of epilepsy.

A year and a half ago, I was asked to be the Spokesperson for the Epilepsy Foundation of America (EFA). Our son with epilepsy was completely opposed to it. "Why bother?" he said angrily, "People don't get it, anyway." He was also afraid that because I was an actress, his friends might see or hear his name connected with epilepsy in a television or magazine interview.

My other two children, one of whom was crying, said that I hurt their brother every time I talked about it. I should keep quiet, except within our immediate family. I said their brother shouldn't feel any more ashamed of having epilepsy than they should of wearing glasses or having asthma. I told them that secrets about epilepsy or abuse or incest punished the innocent and kept them victims, that God wanted hidden things brought into the light to dispel darkness. We talked about the many ugly things that hide or grow and fester in darkness, ignorance, and superstition.

My husband also was not enthusiastic but agreed, knowing I would stand by our son's right to privacy. He joined me at a national leadership meeting for EFA. It was the first time I had met another mother of a child with epilepsy. The tears came against my will. It was also the first time my husband had met another father. Meeting other parents and a group of people connected because of epilepsy was the beginning of many healthful changes that have followed. *Do it.*

I have found that epilepsy upsets the equilibrium of the family system and affects each member socially, psychologically, and financially. It is not simply a medical problem.

When my son developed epilepsy, I grieved over the loss of his potential and the physical, mental, and emotional pain he had to endure. Was he picking up on my anxiety? It seemed as though everything I knew he needed was a fight to get from my husband—a teacher, a school, a coach. I grieved over the loss of quality time with my other children. I was overwhelmed by the responsibility of managing everything alone. The chaos that would erupt before school, at night, or on weekends because of a seizure was like nothing my girlfriends, my neighbors, or other mothers were experiencing. It became obvious that they thought I was not a good organizer or disciplinarian or that I had monstrous children. I stopped talking with all of them about the very thing I needed to share the most.

These experiences taught me that *there is still a tremendous amount of ignorance, fear, and prejudice about this condition.* Almost every person you know and every person you meet must be educated about it before they can be supportive. One person cannot do it alone. If you and your spouse cannot do it together or trade off, then get a friend or relative to help. Keep trying to share the learned information.

Mothers need consistent help with the child's medical appointments and homework. Not only do the other children need their mother's time, but it's not healthful for mother and child to be tied to each other for such long periods, day in and day out. It becomes difficult for the mother to separate herself emotionally from the child, or the child from the mother. It can lead to overprotectiveness of the child, which can cause behavioral problems in the child and clinical depression in the mother.

If you have doubts about the diagnosis, get a second opinion! Ask questions and get clarification. Take notes or tape your doctor's answers. It will be hard for you to absorb everything in the beginning. It's also a good way of sharing information if both parents were not present.

Sometimes doctors will try to put you off with "Let's cross that bridge when or if we come to it." My experience has taught me that it is better to be prepared. Don't be hysterical when you phone the doctor, but don't be intimidated either. Understand the difference between emergency—now, urgent, today—and the doctor's phone list—up to 2 weeks.

There are several important questions to ask your doctor:

1. What kind of seizures does our child have?
2. How do we recognize them? (You'll learn more about recognizing seizures by reading this book than by any description from your doctor.)

3. What should we do and how should we respond when seizures happen?
4. How do we administer and adjust medications? (Both parents must understand something of the nature, dangers, and dosages of the drugs.)
5. How should the dosage change if our child is sick or not as active?
6. What do we do if our child misses one, two, or three pills?
7. What do we do if the child has an allergic reaction to the medication?
8. What are the dangers of not monitoring the levels of the drug through regular blood tests?
9. What is the function of the part of the brain where my child's seizures occur?
10. What is my child's potential level of development?

You need to know that there are specialists in the field of epilepsy who specialize even further than other doctors. If your child's case is complicated, you may need a specialist. There are pediatricians, neurologists, pediatric neurologists, pediatric epileptologists (epilepsy specialists for children), and neurosurgeons. There is also the possibility that your child may need other professionals, such as a nutritionist or neuropsychologist. Even a well-adjusted family may need a psychiatrist or psychologist as part of their support team.

Make changes if you need to, starting today. How your family functioned before the diagnosis is an important factor in how it copes with the crisis. The family's adjustment has a profound effect on how your child reacts. Just remember that strong family support can help change the attitudes and behaviors of the less enlightened people in your community.

Epilepsy has been pushed underground because of lack of knowledge and superstition. The sooner you educate yourself, the better you will be at informing, educating, and fighting for your child with relatives, friends, neighbors, coaches, teachers, principals, nurses, camp counselors, and various doctors. The earlier you do it, the more support you *all* will have.

Our son has been off seizure medicine for 3 months and appears to be seizure-free. I was one of the lucky mothers whose child's seizures were controlled. But even so, having a child with epilepsy is complicated and hard to deal with. My prayer is that you and your family will take to heart the revelations shared by the parents, children, and doctors in this book.

Jaime Lyn Bauer

PREFACE

The Brainstorms Family: Epilepsy on Our Terms is the third in a series of books that describe seizures and epilepsy in plain terms. The first book, *Brainstorms: Epilepsy in Our Words* (Raven Press, 1993), contained many first-person accounts of adults with epilepsy. The second book, *The Brainstorms Companion: Epilepsy in Our View* (Raven Press, 1995), provided the perspectives of family members, friends, and associates of adults with seizures, as well as guidelines for living safely with seizures.

Soon after the publication of *The Brainstorms Companion: Epilepsy in Our View,* parents of children with epilepsy began to clamor for another book that focused specifically on children with epilepsy and their parents. Therefore, I set out, in conjunction with two of my colleagues, Drs. Georgia Montouris and John Pellock, to collect the stories of children with seizures and their parents. I received additional contributions from the parent network of the Epilepsy Association of Massachusetts and past recipients of the Winning Kid award of the Epilepsy Foundation of America (EFA). Their stories have all been assembled in this book. As in the previous two books, the detail found in many of these descriptions is exceptional.

The primary purpose of this book is to present, in understandable terms, information about childhood seizures from people who are directly affected. It is intended for children with epilepsy, their families, and their social network. Readers will have an opportunity to develop insight into their own situations based on the words of other children and parents who are coping with many similar issues. We hope that these insights will strengthen communication within families affected by epilepsy, and between families and health care providers. Additional goals of this book are to dispel feelings of isolation and despair and to help initiate the processes of healing and acceptance.

The volume is divided into four sections. The first section, written by Dr. Pellock, is an introduction to epilepsy and to the different types of seizures that occur in children. Specific recommendations about diagnostic tests and treatment are beyond the scope of this book. These topics should be discussed with primary care physicians and neurologists.

The second section consists of seizure descriptions. Each description or set of descriptions is numbered. At the beginning of each passage, the relationship of the writer to the child with seizures is given. For example, if "mother" is found at the beginning of a description, the contributor is the mother of a child with seizures. Children who write about their own seizures are identified by their age. There are several drawings by children with epilepsy as well.

The third section is a guide for schoolteachers and parents. It was written by William Murphy, the Executive Director of the Epilepsy Association of Massachusetts, who has extensive experience in providing epilepsy education in the classroom.

The fourth section, written by Dr. Montouris, is a glossary of the medical terms referred to in the book, many of which may be new to readers.

Appendix I is a list of EFA affiliates. Appendix II contains the names of pertinent books, publications, and videotapes. Appendix III lists the EFA Winning Kids who wrote stories for this book, as well as information about the artwork that appears in the center of the book.

At the end of the book is an index, which consists of two parts: "Feelings" and "Seizure Observations." Each of these sections is further divided for children and parents. The number next to each entry in the index refers to the selection number, not the page number, which is found above the beginning of each passage.

The Brainstorms Family: Epilepsy on Our Terms reveals the terror, uncertainty, and frustration felt by children and parents after the initial seizure and diagnosis of epilepsy, and the ongoing trials, tribulations, and triumphs of coping with seizures, medication schedules and side effects, health care providers and hospitals, schoolmates, siblings, relatives, and friends. We are indebted to the children and parents who bravely recorded their experiences so that others could learn and benefit from them. Their words often reveal an inspiring sense of purpose and conviction, and an unfettered understanding of what is truly important in life.

Peter Van Haverbeke of the EFA was instrumental in contacting the parents of EFA Winning Kids. I would like to thank Jaime Lyn Bauer, celebrity spokesperson for the EFA, for writing the foreword. I greatly admire her advocacy for people with seizures and their parents. My special thanks go to Cecile Davis, whose hard work and diligence made this project possible. I would like to acknowledge the enthusiastic support of Lippincott–Raven Healthcare. Thanks to Cathy Somer for her editorial assistance. Dr. Carl Stafstrom was helpful in gathering stories from his patients. Finally, I would like to recognize the support of Kell Cannon and the CIBA–Geigy Corporation for their distribution of this book and its predecessors, continuing the commitment made by Cynthia Joyce, who was an enthusiastic driving force behind the *Brainstorms* series.

I invite those who would like to share their own stories or their reactions to this book to write to me in care of Beth Israel Hospital, Comprehensive Epilepsy Center, 330 Brookline Avenue, Boston, Massachusetts 02215.

Steven C. Schachter, M.D.
August 14, 1996

CONTRIBUTORS

Steven C. Schachter, M.D. *Director of Clinical Research, Comprehensive Epilepsy Center, Beth Israel Hospital; Assistant Professor of Neurology, Harvard Medical School, Boston, Massachusetts*

Georgia D. Montouris, M.D. *Medical Director, Epi-Care Center, Semmes-Murphey Clinic; Clinical Instructor, Neurology, University of Tennessee, Memphis, Tennessee*

John M. Pellock, M.D. *Chairman, Division of Child Neurology, Director, Comprehensive Epilepsy Clinics, MCV Hospitals; Professor of Neurology, Pediatrics, Pharmacy, and Pharmaceutics, Medical College of Virginia, Virginia Commonwealth University, Richmond, Virginia*

Jaime Lyn Bauer *Celebrity spokesperson for the Epilepsy Foundation of America; actress, star of television and the stage, Studio City, California*

William Murphy *Executive Director, Epilepsy Association of Massachusetts, Boston, Massachusetts*

Epilepsy and Seizures in Children

John M. Pellock

"I'm not sure but sometimes she just seems to stare out into space."
"He fell down hard, got stiff and shook all over. He couldn't breathe and got blue. . . It was terrible! . . . Help us, please."

EPILEPSY DEFINED

Childhood epilepsy comes in many forms. An otherwise bright, alert, and very intelligent child may have only brief staring spells, whereas another child with other handicaps may have prolonged convulsions. Therefore, what epilepsy means to an individual depends on the person he or she knows or has heard about with epilepsy. Seizure types, their causes, and illnesses that may be associated with seizures all influence what we think about when we attempt to define epilepsy.

A seizure is a symptom that the brain is malfunctioning. It is a clinical event. This malfunction may be transient and may never recur, or it may be the sign of a permanent disability that will bring many more seizures. Because different areas of the brain can produce seizures, they may take on very different characteristics in each child or adult. The term *epilepsy* is used to refer to a group of disorders marked by recurrent seizures. Most children with epilepsy have one or only a few types of seizures. However, as children grow and mature, the behavior that characterizes their seizures may vary. In some children, new seizure types appear as they grow older, whereas in others the seizures eventually disappear and they are said to have "grown out of their seizures." The eventual course of a child's epilepsy is frequently related to the cause of the seizures.

Each seizure represents a sudden, excessive firing of nerve cells in the brain, and is like an electrical storm, with the seizure itself being the way the body reacts to that storm. The nerve cells may be so exhausted after the seizure that they

3

become quiescent, which accounts for the long period of post-seizure confusion and sleepiness. The feature that all types of seizures share is that they are symptoms of brain dysfunction.

CAUSES OF EPILEPSY

Seizures occur for many reasons: brain cells that become unstable because of trauma, brain cells (called *neurons*) that develop abnormally, chemical causes, inflammation and infection, drugs and intoxicating substances, tumors, or strokes. Some patients apparently inherit epilepsy. Today it is suspected that neurotransmitters and the receptors in the neuron that allow these brain chemicals to function may be altered in certain persons with inherited types of epilepsy. In adults, seizures are more likely to be caused by tumors or stroke, whereas in children these causes are much less likely than hereditary or genetic ones. Nevertheless, medical personnel should conduct a full investigation when a child manifests seizures.

About half of people with epilepsy have seizures resulting from an identifiable cause. These are called *symptomatic* seizures because the seizures are symptomatic of a known brain condition. In many children, however, a cause is suspected but cannot be proved. The word *cryptogenic* refers to seizures due to suspected but unproven causes. Seizures that are genetic are termed *idiopathic* or *primary*. In the idiopathic forms of epilepsy, the tendency for epilepsy to develop is inherited, although not everyone who inherits this trait actually has seizures. Environmental factors, such as flickering lights or sleep deprivation, may trigger seizures in those who are genetically susceptible.

TYPES OF SEIZURES

For diagnostic purposes, it is extremely important for the physician to have a description of a child's seizures from someone who has witnessed one or more events. This description of the event, plus the findings on the electroencephalogram (EEG), allows the physician to classify the seizure type. Proper classification enables the physician to plan appropriate medical testing and choose the most appropriate antiepilepsy medications for treatment of the child's condition.

The types of seizures that occur in children can be classified into two broad categories according to how they begin in the brain: generalized and partial seizures. The broad category of generalized seizures includes absence, myoclonic, atonic, and tonic–clonic types. *Absence* seizures are staring spells. *Myoclonic* seizures cause sudden jerks of the body. *Infantile spasms,* which occur during early infancy, are believed to be a type of myoclonic seizure. *Atonic* seizures, or drop attacks, are characterized by a sudden slumping of the whole body or of the head. Some children with atonic seizures fall and should wear helmets to help protect them from injuring their heads when they fall. *Tonic–clonic* seizures are characterized by stiffening of the body (tonic phase) followed by repetitive jerking of the body (clonic phase). This type of seizure is also called a *convulsion;* in the past it was termed a *grand mal* seizure. Some children may have seizures in which only tonic or clonic activity occurs.

Partial seizures begin in one part of the brain and are subclassified into two types. In *simple partial* seizures, consciousness is not altered. These seizures may consist of brief symptoms such as smells, tastes, or feelings of fear, anger, or excitement, and they may also be represented by jerking of an arm, a leg, or the face. *Complex partial* seizures may have these same symptoms but are also marked by a confusional state because more of the brain is involved. Both kinds of partial seizures may then progress over seconds to become convulsions (technically known as partial seizures with secondary generalization). The term *status epilepticus* is used to describe seizures of any type that are prolonged or recurrent over a period of time without full recovery between seizures.

Even having excellent descriptions of the event, it is sometimes difficult for the physician to differentiate between different types of seizures coming from different parts of the brain because they may cause similarly appearing clinical behavior, such as staring spells. In these cases, the findings on the EEG, coupled with the description of the behavior, may allow a more precise definition of the seizure type.

EPILEPSY SYNDROMES

The seizure type is defined by the behavior during the event and by the EEG findings. Although many patients have only one type of seizure, some have two or more types or a single type with some variations in behavior during different spells. Epilepsy *syndromes* are defined not only by the description of the seizure(s) observed but also by such other features as age at seizure onset, cause (etiology), likelihood of inheritance, part of the brain involved, other associated neurologic abnormalities, factors that precipitate events, frequency and severity of seizures, natural course and prognosis for seizure control or worsening, and EEG findings during and between seizures. Syndromes are classified by the predominant seizure types (partial versus generalized) and the suspected cause (idiopathic, symptomatic, or cryptogenic). The epilepsy syndrome, in essence, describes the patient's entire condition.

Several epilepsy syndromes are well known. The most common one is febrile seizures, which typically consist of short, benign convulsions in young children (usually below the age of 5 years) when they have a fever. These children rarely have epilepsy later in life. The syndrome of childhood absence epilepsy affects school-aged children and consists of brief, generalized absence seizures (staring spells) many times daily. Previously called *petit mal,* these seizures respond very well to medications. Children with the Lennox–Gastaut syndrome have multiple seizure types, are retarded, and have very abnormal EEGs. Whereas febrile seizures and childhood absence epilepsy are believed to be familial or inherited, the Lennox–Gastaut syndrome is symptomatic of an injured or malformed brain.

Identifying a child's epilepsy syndrome allows the patient, family, and physician to plan appropriately for the initial and subsequent evaluations of the child, to choose the correct medication (if deemed necessary), to plan for the length of therapy, to determine the need for ongoing medical testing, and to estimate the outcome. Some syndromes, however, are identified only after a child is followed for a number of years.

MEDICAL TREATMENT

Epilepsy in a child may be manifest in combination with many other symptoms and may have a variety of causes. The physician will evaluate the historical report of the events, examine the patient to search for any associated neurologic symptoms or disorders, obtain an EEG, and frequently do other testing, such as brain imaging. Imaging studies such as magnetic resonance imaging (MRI) and computed tomography (CT) allows medical professionals to see the structure of the brain and search for abnormalities. Brain imaging does not enable the physician to determine whether seizures are present but may help to identify possible causes of the epilepsy. Brain imaging studies in the majority of children with epilepsy are normal.

After the diagnosis is made, a treatment plan should be implemented whereby the child usually receives medication regularly for a prolonged period. A few types of seizures that occur in childhood are so benign that long-term therapy may not be recommended (e.g., febrile seizures, some types of partial seizures). The child should take medication daily as prescribed by the physician. Side effects such as dizziness, drowsiness, and incoordination are not uncommon. More serious side effects, such as rashes or harmful effects on the child's liver, bone marrow, or blood cells, are unusual but may necessitate immediate medical attention or emergency treatment. As children with seizures become older they should be made aware of the side effects that are possible and the importance of telling their parents and physicians about them if they occur. Both children and their caretakers should freely discuss the good and bad aspects of taking medications daily. Alternative medications may be available, but almost all anticonvulsants produce some side effects in some persons.

Many children, especially those without other medical conditions or neurologic handicaps, may be able to stop taking medication after a few years, but it is important that this decision be made only after careful discussion and consideration of all the consequences. Patients who stop taking anticonvulsants should discuss with their physicians whether to curtail their driving, because stopping medications may lead to further seizures.

OVERVIEW

The impact of epilepsy varies from person to person and from family to family, as expressed vividly in the many reports from children and their parents that are contained in this book. Dealing with the disability of epilepsy and with related disabilities makes every decision an individual one and is sometimes complicated. The goals of therapy are to stop all seizures while allowing no side effects and to promote the best possible quality of life for the child. Through education and advances in the study of epilepsy, the use of new medications, and open discussions of the disorder, many people now find their entire lifestyle much improved, even if their epilepsy continues. Few people with epilepsy are cured, but most children can lead a normal or near-normal life.

Seizure Descriptions

❖ ❖ ❖ ❖ ❖

1

(Age 11) Because I have nocturnal epilepsy, no one has ever actually seen me have a seizure except my parents. No one knows I have epilepsy unless I tell them or they see my photograph on our county epilepsy poster. Then they ask me why I'm on the poster and I tell them about me and epilepsy.

When I go to bed, I just feel normal. About an hour after I go to bed, I have a seizure. I can't feel the seizure coming on because I'm asleep. During the seizure, I jerk a lot and I feel like I can't breathe, like I'm choking on something. No matter how hard I try, I can't stop the seizure. One time I was at a sleepover with my friend. I had a seizure in bed. My friend didn't know what was happening to me. She just kept telling me to stop moving.

After I have a seizure, I have a headache. The day after my first seizure, I got very sick and had a bad headache. I also had a bruise on my face from falling. I felt disoriented and my speech was slurred. The after effects of my seizures were most severe the first time. They have gradually lessened.

The doctor has told me that I will probably grow out of my seizure condition. I would like to stop having seizures so I could stop taking medication, getting blood tests, and seeing doctors every 2 months.

(Mother) My daughter Lauren has nocturnal epilepsy, which means that her seizures occur only while she is asleep. She began having them suddenly when she was $8\frac{1}{2}$ years old, and they always occurred within a hour or two of her going to bed. My husband and I have never seen her just before a seizure, so we have no way of knowing if there are signs of the impending seizure or not.

In fact, we completely misdiagnosed the first seizure. We had just gone to bed when we heard her fall on the floor. We went to her room to find her on the floor in a puddle of urine. Thinking she had tried to go to the bathroom, fell, and had an accident, we helped her up, cleaned her, and put her back to bed. The next day she was uncharacteristically tired and lethargic.

Exactly 1 month later I awoke to a choking sound coming from Lauren's bedroom. We found Lauren having what must have been a seizure. I held her head in my lap and talked to her quietly until the seizure ended and she went back to sleep. I remained calm and thought to myself that she must be having a seizure. It lasted about a minute. I believe I was more surprised than frightened. I also felt helpless because I couldn't make it stop.

The next day, my husband, Carl, and I discussed the situation. I told Carl that I thought Lauren had suffered a seizure but he displayed the classic parental denial and dismissed it, saying she just probably had a bad dream.

Maybe a couple of weeks later, the same thing reoccurred, but his time I woke Carl so that he could witness what was happening. Carl, an EMT, recognized that Lauren was having a typical convulsive seizure; stiff limbs, jerky movements, eyes open but unfocused, drooling, and loss of bladder control. The duration of the seizure was 1 to 2 minutes, after which Lauren was conscious but disoriented and complained of a slight headache. Within 15 minutes she went back to sleep and slept until morning. The following day she again displayed the exhaustion and lethargy she had shown the day after "the accident" a month earlier.

As parents, we now knew we had a child who needed medical attention so we went first to our family doctor, who did the initial testing. The fear came later when she was scheduled for a CT scan to see if she had a brain tumor. Then I was scared and prayed for her to be all right. Much to our relief, the CT scan ruled out a brain tumor, and Lauren had no more seizures for almost 8 months. Then, however, she had several seizures in fairly quick succession, so we took her to a pediatric neurologist who diagnosed her as having nocturnal epilepsy and recommended medication. Again displaying some denial tendencies, Carl took her out of town for a second opinion, which was identical to the first, right down to the drug of choice. Lauren's dosage was adjusted and she has been seizure-free for 2 years.

I do fear for her future and wonder if she will grow out of her seizure condition. I read what I can about epilepsy, using the EFA newspaper as a source. I want to be informed about new drugs, treatments, and discoveries, knowing that Lauren may have this condition throughout her life.

(Father) It was a shock. I've been an EMT for almost 10 years and have seen some pretty awful things. I was in the Vietnam war, and more recently saw my own son die. But to realize that my lovely daughter, perfect in every way, had something wrong with her was as big a shock as anything I've ever experienced. To see this young lady who had been blessed, and had blessed us, with everything a human could want for the first $8\frac{1}{2}$ years of life (beauty, brains, and excellent health) suddenly lying there stiff, jerking uncontrollably, drooling, staring blankly, and wetting the bed was a tremendous blow to me.

My perfect daughter was not perfect. I made an attempt at denial, but I could not deny what my eyes had seen. I'm sure there was also a good-sized dose of self-pity.

After a brain tumor was ruled out, I felt like a load had been lifted off my shoulders. All the self-pity suddenly disappeared during our first visit to the pediatric neurologist, when I saw some of the other patients in the waiting room and realized that our problems were very small potatoes compared to those of some other people. I was still very concerned about the idea of Lauren being on medication, and that is why I took her out of town for the second opinion. When both doctors completely agreed, I felt much better.

The only concern I have now is whether Lauren will someday, and hopefully soon, be able to get off the medication. If, however, that day never comes and she has to be on medication indefinitely, then I'm okay with that. We are still blessed with a perfect daughter who just has to take a couple of little pills each day.

2

❖ ❖ ❖ ❖ ❖

(Age 12)   I'm Becky. I'm 12 years old and I have epilepsy. It is hard to tell my friends that I have epilepsy. Every year someone from the Epilepsy Association comes to talk about epilepsy to my class, but I don't tell everybody I have epilepsy and that I am a Winning Kid because I don't want to brag about it. By being a Winning Kid, I have learned a lot about epilepsy and I'm not shy when I talk to people I don't know. When I have to talk in front of people, I talk loud and clear. If you have epilepsy, too, remember—it's not just you!

(Mother)   My experience of being thrown into the world of epilepsy began on a freeway exit on the way to the airport. My daughter, Becky, my son, Tony, and I were going to the airport to pick up my husband, Patrick.

Becky had fallen asleep. I was on the off ramp when Tony and I heard this horrible noise coming from the back seat. I turned to see Becky thrashing around and making these noises. Somehow I pulled to the side of the road and turned the car off. I grabbed Becky from the seat and started to pound her back. I was sure she was choking on something. I just started screaming and screaming. People stopped on both sides of the off ramp to help. I was very lucky that one of the people who stopped was a nurse who knew exactly what to do. She took Becky from me, placed her on her side, and put her jacket under Becky's head. While all this was going on many wonderful people stayed with Tony and me. A young man selling flowers on the street corner dropped his flowers, jumped a fence, and called 911.

When the seizure was finished, Becky was briefly unconscious. Again, I screamed, but this time because I thought she had died. In those brief seconds I thought I had lost my daughter. The nurse called me over to have me put my hand on Becky's chest to feel her heart beating. What a relief! But this relief was short-lived because when Becky became conscious she could not see me. She said "Mommy, I can't see you." This also lasted only seconds, but in a matter of minutes I went from a daughter who I thought was choking, to one who just died, to one who was blind. Some very intense emotions occurred during those minutes.

We now know what to do if Becky has a seizure. I now no longer scream but I will always worry. It is a frustrating thing for parents to be unable to "cure" their child. I will continue to encourage Becky to be or do whatever she wants, because she is a "Winning Kid" whether she has epilepsy or not. She can do anything with my blessings. Children with epilepsy should be encouraged to have dreams just like everyone.

Don't take their dreams away.

3

(Mother) The first feeling I always have when my daughter has a seizure is disappointment, because I never give up hope that she will stop having seizures. I always want my daughter to know that I am with her and that she is safe. It is a heartbreaking experience. We make the best of it and face life as it comes.

4

❖ ❖ ❖ ❖ ❖

(Age 8)   Hi, I'm Tammaron. I have epilepsy and seizures. It is very hard for me because other kids make fun of me. But they don't understand. The medicine I am on is helping me to handle my problem better. I have a wonderful doctor and lovely nurses. I am starting to do better with the embarrassment of having seizures.

With God on my side and the help of my doctors and nurses I will make it.

Love you all.

5

❖ ❖ ❖ ❖ ❖

(Mother)   I was paralyzed with fear on witnessing my son's first seizure, which happened when he was 5 years old. Despite working in the nursing profession for 26 years, my medical skills seemed useless. I was able to detach myself enough to dial 911 and inform the dispatcher that David was having continuous seizures. The seizure seemed to last forever. Forever turned out to be 5 minutes. I literally felt as if his life was slipping through my hands and I was helpless to stop the process.

In the two years since his first major seizure, the enemy—epilepsy—has kept a relentless grip on our family. David's father, brother, and I have become hypervigilant and quite skilled at detecting impending seizure activity. Because David is severely mentally challenged, he is unable to report an aura or describe his symptoms after a seizure. Early on, David's neurologist advised us not to let his seizure disorder consume us, but we battle with this. David's epilepsy has disturbed our family equilibrium.

Our family has therefore adapted to his condition and become first responders when David has an emergency. Last summer, while we were vacationing in Maryland, David had a cluster of seizures that necessitated a trip to the emergency room. The ER physician, impressed with our knowledge of epilepsy, jokingly remarked that David traveled with his own rescue squad.

In the back of our minds, there is always the fear that David's life will be shortened because of his seizures.

6

(Age 17) It is almost a year since my diagnosis of epilepsy. Well, to put it mildly, living with epilepsy is no piece of cake. However, knowing what I'm living with is easier to deal with than not knowing.

My first experiences were strange. I was 16 years old and I would have these strange sensations. At first it was just like everyone was looking at me. Then it felt like I was trying to remember something but could only remember fragments, sort of like "deja vu." My first doctor said I was having migraines. He had some tests run—I forget what it's called, but it's where they put wires on your head. I continued to have these "things," as they came to be called.

During one of my basketball games, I sat down on the court. My teammates told me later that the referee thought I was doing that to protest a call. They got me off the court, though I don't remember that. I do remember sitting on the bench and having people try to talk to me, but I couldn't understand what they were saying.

My mom heard of another doctor. I went to see her and she

told me that I probably had epilepsy, but she wanted to monitor me in the hospital to make sure. That scared me. I've always been perfectly healthy. But the thing that upset me the most was that two of my uncles had died from seizure-related accidents. One of them was my godfather.

I didn't want to go to the hospital because my school is very strict about not allowing absences. My teachers, however, agreed to treat my hospital stay as an excused absence.

My sister came in from out of town to help my mom stay with me while I was admitted. I don't think I minded the hospital. I think it was interesting and I would like to be a doctor some day. I was surprised at the amount of flowers I received from family and friends. I had wires on my head the entire time so they could monitor my brain activity. I laughed when they gave me a bike pedal device to use in bed. They gave it to me because I seemed to have my things when I performed physical activity. I pedaled for 2 days until I finally had a thing. My doctor told my family and me that the thing was a seizure. I think they were as happy as I was to finally know what it was. However, I think the word "epilepsy" scared my mom. I got started on medication.

I went to my class retreat later that year. We had just finished the official eating and were going in to talk. I sat down and waited. The next thing I remember was thinking how neat it was that they got the paramedics to come talk to us. Then they came over to me. I couldn't understand what they were saying and they took me to the ambulance and gave me some oxygen and left. My parents came and took me home for the night. My friends told me the next day that I had a convulsion. They said I started shaking. One of my friends who had some first-aid classes made everyone move and handled the situation. I had never done anything before that night except stare when I had a seizure. I found out it was a reaction to the medicine that caused it. I think I gave my class a real scare.

The seizures themselves are not too bad. I usually feel that I'm trying to remember something but I can't. Then I stare. I usually put my right hand to my face. After it, I have trouble understanding what people are saying to me. My seizures usually occur during some type of physical activity (like when I'm playing a sport), but not necessarily. I am most likely to have them during menstruation or ovulation.

Living with epilepsy is hard work, but the seizures are probably easier to deal with than are some of my medicines. My second medicine made me sleep so much that I could hardly stay awake to do my homework. I could fall asleep anywhere, anytime. I even fell asleep walking once. I slept in every single one of my classes at least twice. Chemistry was one class I could barely stay awake for. My mom tried everything to help me stay awake to study for my exams. The medicine, along with all the others I have tried, didn't work.

Another medicine made my stomach hurt. For 2 weeks during the summer I couldn't do anything but lie down on the sofa. That's really hard for someone like me who always wants to be doing something.

One of the most difficult things I've had to deal with is trouble with my memory. My seizures occur in the part of the brain commonly called "the memory bank." I have a difficult time remembering things. I have trouble remembering what happened in the part of the book I just read, who I just met, what I was supposed to do, what I was supposed to know for a history test, and just about everything else.

But the worst part of this is that in my state, a person diagnosed with epilepsy has to be 6 months seizure-free before he or she can drive again. This bit of news is probably the worst thing you can tell a person who has been driving for only 9 months.

Coping with all of this has been hard and frustrating. I think I'm on my fifth or sixth medicine, and I had a seizure 2 days ago. I now cannot drive for another 6 months. It is really hard for me to rely on other people to drive me everywhere. Sometimes this gets me depressed, but my friends help me to go on. My friends have dealt with this well. I still have the same friends that I had before my experience at the class retreat.

This has been particularly hard on my mom. I think it worries her that I haven't been successful with my medication. I think it hurts her that this is one thing that she can't help me with.

Epilepsy, however, has not stopped me. I have not let my seizures or my medicine stop me from playing sports. I am on the varsity soccer, basketball, and softball teams. During this past soccer season I had to be taken off the field a couple of times because I was just staring. However, I would ask to be put back in when I could comprehend what was going on.

I am currently ranked first in my class and have recently been named a National Merit Semi-Finalist. I think my sense of humor and the thought that somebody up there is looking out for me helps me.

7

(Parents)   After years of our son trying one drug after another without success, we began to wonder which was worse, the seizures or the side effects from the medication. Our son had experienced sickness because of incorrect drug levels, weight fluctuations, mood swings, lack of friends, and an inability to focus in school. We had constant meetings with teachers trying to convince them not to give up on him. Above all else was our sense of frustration in dealing with his short-term memory loss. However, with each trip to the hospital after he lapsed into continuous seizures, we knew we had no choice but to continue our quest for a miracle cure.

Finally, in desperation, we turned to surgery, but this also was unsuccessful. Our biggest disappointment of all lies in our experience with the specialist who was recommended by our local neurologist. We arrived for our first appointment with our hopes, fears, and dreams built up over years of sleepless nights and an equal number of shed tears. We prayed this would be the answer we were looking for. Yet that institution and most of their doctors to whom we looked for help were much more concerned about how much our insurance company would pay rather than what course of action would be best for our child. This lack of compassion and concern left us heartbroken and in disbelief.

Many times, dealing with our son's condition is like having a door slammed in our face, whether by the doctors, the school system, or even the parents of other children.

But we refuse to give up on our son and we're still searching. Does anyone *really* care?

8

❖ ❖ ❖ ❖ ❖

(*Mother*)   I have a beautiful daughter named Andrea. She is now 29 years old. She has had seizures since she was 5 years old and has been on many medications without success. We believe that her seizures are related to birth complications. Right after she was born she had a seizure and turned blue in the nursery. They did not expect her to live. She was my only daughter (I also have three sons), and I prayed very hard for her recovery.

She eventually did well and had all the normal developmental milestones of a young child until the day she had her first seizure and fell.

Despite the new diagnosis of epilepsy, I was so full of hope and energy. I devoured as much literature as I could. I tried to educate anyone who came in contact with Andrea, including her friends in the lower grades. I volunteered as much as possible while raising my three sons and taking care of a husband who had to work two jobs to support us.

In the early years of her epilepsy, Andrea's seizures began with hysterical laughing spells. Then she would slump to the ground. After that, she would get up and not remember what had happened. I was surprised when it first happened, and only became alarmed and frightened when it happened a second and third time.

She then progressed to having seizures that involved her slumping to the floor as though she were falling asleep. We would hold her and make sure that she was safe, and then wait it out. She never had or gave us any warning. They occurred on a daily basis so I had to be very vigilant as far as her play activity and school and home environments were concerned. Instead of making her wear an uncomfortable helmet, I made her stuffed hats that matched her clothes. It seems that her childhood was spent in and out of hospitals, trying out new medications and having painful tests to try to find out why this was happening and why we couldn't stop it.

As she grew up and changed medications, her seizures became more active and turned into convulsions. She began to have sudden falls preceding the convulsions, and this was very frightening. We were very concerned that she would be seriously injured as a result of these falls. There was never any warning preceding these falls, and they could occur even if we were right beside her. I made sure that when we went out I held her hand at all times so I could monitor the slightest of movements. We also changed the environment in the house, such as installing wall-to-wall carpeting everywhere and upholstered furniture with no corners and/or sharp edges. In addition, I required her to sit down in a chair as soon as she entered a room, to minimize the chance of injury.

The seizures lasted from 15 seconds to 1 minute and caused very violent shaking of her entire body. The longer seizures caused her lips and fingernails to turn blue because she did not breathe adequately. When she stopped seizing, her eyes and head continued to move, and sometimes her arms would come up, as if she were going to have another seizure, and then fall back down. This could last up to an hour afterwards. Other times she would have 5-second seizures after the first one and then fall asleep. She could sleep for an hour or less, depending on the situation. There were times when she could continue an activity after having a convulsion, and other times when she wasn't able to do anything.

I soon realized that the seizures were beginning to exact a mental toll on Andrea. The school system would not allow her to stay in the regular classroom with her friends but instead sent her to another school with a separate room set aside for handicapped children. This devastated her emotionally. She was approaching puberty without her friends, knowing that she could not learn as well or keep up with them. Her seizures also caused loss of coordination, and she lost the ability to do things she once could do easily. She had to relearn tasks over and over again.

This caused her to be depressed and feel unworthy. For a long time, she refused to look at herself in the mirror. I took her shopping for clothes, I fixed her hair pretty, I tried everything to spark interest in herself. But she just wanted to die. I became her therapist, her friend, her nurse, and her companion as well. There were many nights that I held her in my arms and cried with her. Through love, understanding, and therapy she came out of this phase.

This past year and a half have been the hardest time of all. She has been hospitalized twice and each time was put into a drug-induced coma to stop her seizures. She had breathed in her own saliva each time and developed pneumonia. We almost lost her.

She did survive, but came out of it totally disabled. I took her home as an invalid. I was not prepared for this, so I set about getting as much therapy at home as my insurance would allow.

Now, after 6 months of very hard and rewarding work, she is beginning to talk and move about and sit up with help. She is still on medication while we wait for some new medication that might help her. Both her doctor and I feel that she will come back a hundred percent over time. She is a very brave, special young woman, and her spirits on the whole have been very good. Andrea's doctor has been very responsive to us and is always there for us as well. He is very kind and caring as well as very knowledgeable.

We know now that she will always need a caretaker and I am very concerned about that. My husband and I do not get to share the time together that most couples have. He will not be able to retire when he might like, either. This saddens me, but I try not to dwell on it and let each day take care of itself. The responsibility of all of this falls mostly on my shoulders, but I recognize that I am the stronger one. I have a lot of patience and will persevere as long as necessary.

I am grateful for a lot of things and I appreciate each day that is good all the more. I, too, need to hear her say "I love you mom" on a regular basis. She said that as soon as she could speak a little. The other day she said "thank you" after I changed her diaper and washed her. I hugged her as hard as I could and told her that she was welcome.

9

(Mother)   Leslie was diagnosed with seizures at birth and has been on medication since that time. In the beginning she had small seizures that consisted of the continuous blinking of her eyes. Leslie's seizures could last for such a long time that it was not easy to determine what was going on before the seizure or what instigated the seizure.

When she was 13, we were driving on our vacation and she went into a convulsion. She was in the back seat of the van and just went into it. It was undoubtedly the most scary situation I have ever experienced. She began shaking all over, her eyes were glazed, she was red as could be, and it was as if she was chewing her tongue. She looked like she was scared to death. When she came out of it, her comment was "I couldn't quit shaking" and she began to cry. She kept saying, "Please don't let me start shaking again."

We cut our vacation short. Leslie experienced another seizure about 1 month later. She had been watching television and had gone to bed at her normal time. After lying in bed, she fell out of the bed and went through four seizures within a 30-minute span. She was admitted to the hospital for observation. She was totally exhausted after going through those seizures.

Watching Leslie have seizures was very frightening for me even though I realized what was taking place. Fortunately, her seizures have now been under control for 2 years. You never want to see a loved one go through something like this.

10

(Mother) Douglas is now 12 years old. He was 8 when he first started having seizures. For a long time we did not know what was wrong with him. In fact, we thought he had a very severe discipline problem. He was easily frustrated, quick to anger, and would blow up at his friends for no apparent reason.

After he had a convulsion early one morning, we finally had some idea of what could be wrong with him. He then had all of the required tests and started on the road to finding the correct dosage of medication to hopefully bring him some relief.

We are now aware of when Douglas may experience a seizure and can tell when his medication levels are off. For instance, 1 to 2 weeks before a seizure he starts to withdraw from participating at school, forgets to turn in homework, and just seems somewhat disassociated with everything. He tends to have his seizure in the early morning, around 5:00 A.M. He then feels bad and sleeps and lies around until about 2:00 P.M. After that, he starts feeling better. For the next week he is still somewhat withdrawn from everything and slowly gets back in the swing of things. During this 2- to 3-week period, Douglas is very easily frustrated, is somewhat difficult to get along with, has poor listening skills, lies around a lot, and plays quietly in his room.

11

MY FEELINGS   *(Age 8)*

I feel scared when I am in the dark.
I feel happy when someone is nice to me.
I feel tired when I run.
I feel brave when I have a blood test.
I feel sad when someone is hurt.
I feel shy when a stranger talks to me.
I feel mad when someone teases me.
I feel silly when someone talks funny.

My name is Marie. I am 8 years old. I am on the ketogenic diet. I had to fast in the hospital. I did not mind that because I wanted to get off my meds.

I love to play with my friends and I try to be nice to my friends, too. I don't kick or hit kids at school like I used to. My room number at school is 108. School is fun. I love math and gym. I love the computer, but we do not have one now.

I love to play bingo, but we always lose at bingo.

(Mother) Thanks for letting me share my experience with you. My daughter Carla Marie is 8 years old. She started having seizures at the age of 14 months. She had six seizures in a 24-hour period. It was on a weekend. The first seizure she had lasted about 20 minutes. I called an ambulance. I was scared beyond words.

The doctor at the hospital found that she had an ear infection and a fever. He prescribed her an antibiotic and told me to call him if I needed to. After five more severe seizures in a 24-hour period, I again called the ambulance. This time the doctor put her on seizure medicine. We went home and she didn't have any more seizures (that I knew of) until her next fever with an ear infection. Unfortunately, she had several ear infections, and every time she had a fever she would have convulsions. Marie had over 50 seizures with fevers. Her arms and legs would shake, her body would jerk, her eyes would go back and forth, or roll back or appear to be dazed. Saliva would bubble out of her mouth. She'd always sleep after those seizures, sometimes for hours.

When Marie was 3 she developed short staring spells. They were well-controlled for a few years on seizure medication. When she was 5 she started having another type of seizure that started very mildly. For the first few weeks she would just stop and put her hand on her nose. Then, a few weeks later, she'd start putting her hand on her nose and do mild mouth movements and swallow. Then she would rush to an adult, look afraid, put her hand on her nose, and put your hand on her nose. At the beginning of the seizure, she would say "My nose is bugging me." They gradually got stronger and stronger. We tried lots of medicines and combinations of medicines, but nothing helped for long. She ended up having surgery for those seizures.

Ten months after surgery she had her first convulsion without a fever. I was sleeping on the couch and she was sleeping on the floor by me. She also had a couple of friends sleeping over on the floor. I woke up and she was repeatedly hitting her face on the floor. When I put her on her side, there was blood on her pillow. Her gums were bruised on one side, and because she cut her tongue a little her tongue looked partially bruised or reddish. The worst thing about that seizure was that there was no fever. I took her temperature a couple of times. I was so disappointed that she didn't have a fever. At least I could help a febrile seizure by getting her fever down, but with no fever I couldn't help her with medicine to bring down her fever. That she could have these major seizures without provocation was pretty disturbing to me to say the least.

I picked Marie up early every day from school during first and second grades. In first grade she often took 30- to 60-minute naps in the nurse's office because she was tired from seizure activity and medicines. She would go back to class when she woke up. If she had a headache I'd pick her up. I got a pager so that I could relax a little and know that I could always be reached. Her classmates and teachers were supportive of her. The epilepsy center put on a puppet show for her class, and I think it was very helpful for the children to learn about epilepsy. In second grade I picked her up early every day because her behavior was so out of control that I thought everybody would appreciate having some peace in the class, and her educational assistant, teacher, and class deserved that, too. And Marie needed it. I knew that she couldn't control her aggressive and violent behavior, though we didn't know if it was seizure activity, medicines, or both that was making her behavior so difficult to control. It was her worst year socially.

Before Marie went on the ketogenic diet, she would sleep in my room so I would at least be there and hopefully wake up when she had a seizure during the night, which she did many nights.

Now Marie has been on the ketogenic diet for 8 months. Her behavior has changed drastically for the better. She's making it through the whole day in school. She's off all her medicines and it's great. For the first time in 7 years we can see what she's like without the medicines, and it's like she's matured a couple of years.

I'll admit she's been the center of everything for years. Because of her problems we put her first. Now that she's off the medications she can do more things, so we expect more from her. It's understandable to me why we spoiled her at times. She went through hell, and that ain't easy for a kid. Now we are un-spoiling her and she's fighting that. I know that it will work out in time.

When Marie first started having seizures, I looked in the phone book and found the Epilepsy Center's number. I called and was relieved to talk with someone who could answer my questions. They sent me information, lent me a shoulder to cry on, hooked me up with other people with epilepsy, and more. The more I learned about epilepsy, the less devastating it was. I know it would have been a lot harder without their support.

People have told me that I must be used to my daughter having seizures because she has them every day. But for me every seizure my daughter has hurts me a little.

I keep myself together the best that I can. Regularly dealing with her seizures and behaviors from the medicines has taken the wind out of my sails. But Marie doesn't let her seizures stop her from doing normal activities like biking, riding on boats, big water slides, and playing on equipment. I worry and protect her as much as I can, but she also needs space, and I'm not going to punish her for having seizures by not letting her do fun stuff. Luckily, it's worked out fine so far.

So there it is. I hope you can find something in this story that can help you.

12

(Age 13)   I'm sorry that I have seizures because I can't play many sports. Sometimes I am OK, but sometimes I'm not! I do not know why I have seizures. Most of the times I have seizures at night! I did not like having surgery because I was asleep most of the time! When I have my blood drawn it is OK. I hate taking my medicine at night.

I wonder, will I be OK?

13

BUTTERFLIES   *(Age 9)*

The butterflies come way down my belly.
They flap and flap their wings. They fly up to my mouth and I try to catch one but it's too late.
My mouth freezes open and my hand shakes too hard.
The butterfly flies away and it's gone.
Until the next butterfly comes.

(*Mother*)   Our daughter was only 2 days old when she had her first seizure. Three hours after we brought home our beautiful, perfect girl, everything we valued, thought was important, or set our dreams and hopes on changed instantly.

We found her blue and rigid and called 911. Everything from that point followed the usual emergency path. We looked at each other and couldn't grasp that this was real. We had, of course, heard of epilepsy and seizures, but *our* baby?

Daddy felt helpless and angry that he couldn't *do* something to stop this. Mommy instantly became the lioness ready to devour anyone who might hurt the cub—physically or emotionally (this has softened to some degree over time, but it's still there).

We grieved for our lost dreams. We knew this child would have a harder road than other children, perhaps not physically, but in other ways. Parents dream their children will have the perfect, easily fulfilled, and charmed lives that they deserve. When our babies are born, we don't anticipate the difficult, often gut-wrenching decisions we may have to make on their behalf.

When she was very young and didn't quite understand what was happening to her, she called seizures "the butterflies," and we still use that phrase even now. It's funny. I always think of seizures when I see a butterfly.

As she grew older, our daughter would often feel butterflies in her stomach just before having a seizure. Once the butterfly sensation starts, the usual (I say usual because her seizures can vary) chain of events follows. At first, her eyes start to look as if she's frightened, but then one eye tips to the side slightly. Then the side of her face twitches and her mouth moves as if she's silently wording "ma, ma, ma" (in my mind, anyway). Her arm shakes and jerks, and often she stumbles around as if she's looking for a way to get out. Then she lets out what sounds like her last earthly breath. She falls to the floor and her whole body becomes rigid. As most of us usually do instinctively, I spot the clock. Will this one last the usual 2 to 5 minutes?

Every second lasts forever. After years of the same scenario, it never really gets easy to deal with. How could I think that it would? A few minutes pass and a shuddery gasp signals the end of this one. She turns into a rag doll and begins to snore. I wipe the spittle from her mouth and kiss her clammy face. And hope that this is her last butterfly.

After the grief of dealing with epilepsy comes the growth. We have embraced our child's disorder as part of what makes her so special, and have encouraged her to do the same. We share our experiences with everyone. We're involved in educating anyone who is willing (or even those who are not) to learn about epilepsy.

Watching her seizures has never become easier, but the moments after are no longer the agonizing "why us" moments. They've become moments of "Thank you, God, for giving us *this* child."

14

(Age 16) My name is Bree. I'm 16 years old. I'm a sophomore in high school and a gymnast, too. But I have a certain kind of condition that affects one in 100 people in the United States. My condition is called epilepsy.

I was diagnosed with two kinds of seizures. During the first kind I sit and stare into space. My eyes roll back in my head, too. This past summer I was diagnosed with the second type of seizure, which causes jerking. My hands jump and, if I have something in my hands, it quickly falls to the floor. While my hands jump, my eyes flutter and I don't know what was going on. While all this goes on, I feel confused. It usually happens when I am tired or when I get up in the morning.

But that was before I was on my medicine. Living with epilepsy is no picnic on the beach. You have some privileges taken away. I can't stay up late anymore and I have to go to bed early at slumber parties, that kind of thing. My friends are kind of leery about me sometimes. They really don't understand how frustrating it is to live with such a tricky condition. I have a friend who also has epilepsy. She can relate to me. Adults treat me like any other person.

My mom feels so helpless. And she can't do anything to help me, so that makes her feel guilty, I think. I sometimes get really frustrated at her because she nags me about sleep, my medicine, or what time I should go to bed. But then I realize that she's doing this to make sure I don't have any more seizures. And I appreciate that. No one believed I was having seizures except my mother.

I'm the one who has to live with epilepsy, and there's nothing I can do about it. I have to cope the best I can and live each day at a time.

15

(Mother) Brittni had just started kindergarten and would come home looking real tired. She would ask for a snack, and before you could get it to her she would be asleep. No matter whether she was sitting or standing, she would just lie down and go to sleep. I thought school was really tiring her out. She had always been very bright and very street-smart, so I was surprised when she didn't just whiz right through school.

And then the seizures started. It is hard to write exactly how I felt when Brittni started having seizures. I rushed her to the hospital and found out she had a brain tumor. I can't express the fear that went through me then. Over time, she went through three different brain surgeries, but still the seizures continued.

She has different kinds of seizures. Sometimes she just sits, stares, and falls asleep. Other times, she jerks, cries, and wets herself. She had to take so much medicine that her mind couldn't handle it all. She finally got tired of it and decided she didn't want to live anymore. Her moods were terrible. Fortunately, she had a wonderful doctor who helped us through all this. Without him I don't know how we would have handled all of her mood swings.

I had worked all my life but suddenly couldn't work anymore because every time I went to work the school would call. They didn't know how to handle Brittni's seizures. They wanted to send her home every time she felt a seizure come on. Besides that, they would just pass her in her subjects even though she couldn't even read or write. They put her in a class with regular kids who made fun of her all the time. It's hard enough to deal with a sick child, but its really hard when people don't try to understand what is going on in that child's head.

Brittni cannot write, but I can tell you how she feels. She is afraid that she won't ever be able to drive, work, or get married and have children. Her whole life has changed. Her seizures scare her and she doesn't want to sleep by herself. A couple of hours before bedtime she sits and worries who is going to sleep with her. She is scared that she will have a seizure in her sleep and die.

She wants to be normal. She loves to dance, so I enrolled her in a dance class. The dance instructor said she was wonderful—a natural! So we bought her dance clothes and an outfit for competition and paid the money. Then he didn't let her dance anymore. No reason—he just stopped having practices. That threw her into a real depression.

I just wish people would try to learn what having epilepsy is really like and what kinds of moods the kids go through. They need to know that epilepsy is not something they're going to catch and, if given the chance, kids with seizures will amaze you with what they are capable of doing. Schools are the worst. They need a lot of education about epilepsy. And they need to know that every time they make a big deal out of someone having a seizure and send the kid home, they are teaching the other kids to have negative reactions to the person with seizures.

Brittni's 4-year-old sister handles her seizures very well. She watches after her big sister. If they are playing outside or taking a bath, she always knows when Brittni is going to have a seizure. She'll come and get me and say, "My Sissy is having a seizure," and she'll help move things out of the way so I can lay her sister down. If a 4-year-old can understand, I think more adults should try.

I just thank God for the people that really understand and try to make a difference in these kids' lives. And I really thank God for my daughter's doctor. He has built more self-confidence in my child than any other person. He sees what she is capable of and he gives her a feeling of self-worth and builds up her confidence so that someday she will have a chance to prove herself.

16

(Age 14) My first seizure occurred at the age of 11 months, or so I was told by my parents. My parents were told that I had a stroke because of an AVM [Editor's note: arteriovenous malformation; see Glossary] and that the stroke caused my seizure. I am now 14 years old.

I experienced another seizure in the third grade at an assembly program. After the program I became confused as to where I was. I returned to my class and put my head on my desk. The teacher couldn't get me all the way awake, so my mom and the school nurse took me to the hospital. I stayed for 2 days.

I didn't have another seizure until seventh grade. I had an intestinal virus with diarrhea and vomiting. During the seizures, I got strangled and really scared my family. My blood level of the seizure medication was real low. I don't remember anything about my seizure, just what my parents told me later. I came to in the hospital.

One day last year, I was dressed and ready for school when my mom sent me to my room and later found me on the floor. My parents took me to the emergency room. I spent the day there. The next day I felt fine. I was up walking, laughing, and talking, and the next day when I woke up I couldn't move because I hurt all over. I guess I had another seizure during the night. I couldn't move for 2 weeks. My parents took me to the doctor several times after that, and this time he gave me two medicines for my seizures.

I used to have trouble walking before the seizures, but now I get really shaky sometimes. I have a home teacher because my school has steps inside and out and plus I'm not walking too good by myself.

Once I had a seizure after returning home from the orthodontist. My big brother took me to get a sandwich and when we returned he said he told me to move so he could close the door. He said I just stood there. He was able to get me into the house and then told mom I was acting strange. He said mom knew what was happening. My mom said that it lasted for a short period of time. I couldn't remember. She said that she asked me if I hurt or how I felt. She said that I told her I didn't hurt but felt sick at the stomach. We called my doctor and she said that I needed to get my levels checked. I hate getting blood drawn because they have to stick me too many times to find my veins. The level of my seizure drug in my blood was in the low range. My mom said that I had another seizure coming out of the doctor's office.

My seizures are short, according to my mom, and I just tremble, move my arms, and get stiff. Mom and my brother call me "sleeping beauty" because I sleep so much after a seizure. I also feel cold a lot. I don't know if this is because of my medicine or seizures.

The seizures really frighten my brother. I wish I didn't have them. I hope my children don't have seizures. I really can't tell when I'm going to have a seizure. I get upset when my family keeps asking me if I'm okay every time that I get real quiet. It makes my mom nervous if I don't answer her when she calls me. My dad helps keep me active. He helps me exercise because I get weak after a seizure. Plus he says I need exercise since I don't get outside too much.

I ask my mom and dad if I'm really going to be all right.

17

❖ ❖ ❖ ❖ ❖

(Parents) We are the parents of a precious little girl. One day in August, all our hopes and dreams changed suddenly. What was once important to us was no longer of great significance.

Our little 4-month-old girl was sleeping so peacefully in her crib while daddy was at work, and her 3-year-old brother and I watched a circus on television. I heard something from her crib, turned on the light, and saw that our little baby was stiff, and then she began jerking and salivating heavily. She was blue in the face and was not breathing. In between breathing for her and calling her doctor and someone to get us to the hospital, I thought she would die in my arms. It was the longest ride of my life. I breathed for her while my father sped us to the hospital. He later told me he knew it was out of our hands and he felt she would die if we didn't get her somewhere fast.

Her first seizure lasted approximately 45 minutes and was diagnosed as an adverse reaction to the DPT shot. She had her second seizure 3 months later. Her early seizures usually occurred in association with illness. At first the doctors thought that they were febrile seizures, but she kept having seizures and they became more frequent, some lasting 20 to 45 minutes. Then, gradually, as medicines were changed and she grew, the seizure frequency, pattern, and duration became more tolerable. We have documented each of her 1,071 seizures to date as to the date, time of day, activity when seizure occurred, description of seizure, duration, dosage of medication, and what happened after the seizure.

Looking back, all of this was completely unexpected. Our daughter had a normal delivery followed by well check-ups as recommended. We had no clue to warn us that our daughter would have an adverse reaction to a DPT shot. Our reactions as parents have changed in some ways and not in other ways. The adjustment our entire family has made is that, with time, we have learned more about epilepsy and feel confident that we can get her through the seizures. But we have not changed in the sense that with each and every seizure we feel so much disappointment and heartfelt sympathy for her. Even so, we always have a glimmer of hope that she won't have another one.

We have experienced all kinds of seizures, varying with types of medications, including continuous seizures, drop attacks, tremors, screams, and states of partial consciousness. As parents we have experienced disappointment with other people—the lack of a helping hand in the aisle of a grocery store and other public places or stares from adults who do not understand her handicap. Her condition often cycles from a few goods days (few seizures) to a few bad days. There have been times when we couldn't let her run around outside, especially if it was hot, because it would lead to a seizure.

The effects of her condition on our family are constant. We are often changing plans and canceling trips, yet as a family we have accepted the effects of seizures on our lifestyle and have made the necessary adjustments. Often only one parent attends the events of our other two children. But we are concerned about the impact of our daughter's condition on our other children. They worry more about their sister than we probably realize. For instance, when our 11-year-old son was in first grade, he would always say that his number one wish or dream was for his sister to be well. We also worry about the perceptions of the friends of our other two children and that they may not include our children in their plans because of their sister with epilepsy.

Some members of our family and some of our friends have accepted our situation, but others have not and exclude us from their "invitation list." With this is mind, we are determined to have as normal a life as possible. We do all we can, such as attending church, going boating, swimming, traveling, bowling, and going to ball games. We treat her as a normal child as much as possible.

Overall, it must be realized that this illness is not a good thing that has happened to our daughter and our family. There are plenty of negatives, but with the knowledge of how seriously and gravely ill she has been in the past, only we and very close family members can see the positives. Our love for our three children outweighs all the adversities. We are always happy that we are together every night.

Our daughter's seizure-free days are days of playfulness, alertness, smiles, and the best of days for our family.

If only there were more.

18

(Mother)   My daughter's first seizure occurred at 4:30 P.M. and lasted for about a minute. She was sitting on the floor in front of the TV having a snack. Suddenly, she stopped chewing—mouth open, cracker half chewed, drooling, staring—and did not answer me. Then as if nothing at all had happened she started to finish her saltines and said, "I am very tired," and slept for several hours afterward.

This began to happen quite often. These staring spells and other episodes of "not answering me" upset me. I thought she was ignoring me but then, by chance, like pieces of a puzzle, it all fell into place. You see, she had other bizarre behaviors. I realized that her tantrums and screaming were her way to let me know about the seizures. She was frightened and frustrated. After she failed all the tests for entrance into kindergarten, I took her to a neurologist, and the EEG and MRI showed that she had suffered two strokes. We knew that she also had a cardiac condition and this turned out to be related to the strokes.

After being placed on seizure medicine, and a year of getting the dose to the correct level, she now is seizure-free. What amazes me is that before the medication was started, she would draw monster faces with lots of teeth. Now she draws happy people. So, *this* was her way of communicating to me.

She doesn't understand what epilepsy is or what a seizure is. In her own words she recently told her school nurse "my mind is not confused now."

She tries hard in school but she does have some learning disabilities. She can write her name now and is learning to read. Now she is in first grade and finds it difficult—these past 2 weeks she has been crying at school—but we all reassure her that it's OK and we're all here to help. I don't feel she should be in the resource room, because her I.Q. is 110! She is an average to above-average individual. But Staci is treated just like every other kid at school. We don't make an issue of it because her seizures are under control.

I also had to educate the teachers. I gave them Epilepsy Foundation of America videos to help them understand seizures. I feel like I'm going down a road that isn't paved and others will follow—it will get smoother eventually.

I would like to thank everyone who works hard for the adults and children with epilepsy.

I understand now.

19

❖ ❖ ❖ ❖ ❖

(Mother) My son and only child, Jonathan Paul, is $10\frac{1}{2}$ years old. For most of those years he has been plagued with an unusual type of epilepsy that has yet to be conquered.

A runny nose and croupy cough when he was 15 months old were the only signs that his health was in jeopardy. To this day I feel guilty that I did not recognize the seizures for what they were. I watched him have these "spells" of odd behavior for 3 days and nights before going to the hospital emergency room. That day, Christmas Eve, he was snatched from my arms and rushed into a large emergency room filled with nurses, doctors, and technicians. The doors to that room were closed in my face, and I began the first of many days and nights pacing a hospital hallway, terrified and blaming myself for what was happening. His father, my husband Calvin, was with me, as were many members of our family and close friends. Yet, *I* felt responsible, for are not mothers seen as the caregivers in the home? The sense of failure was strong, and I have continued to blame myself over the years.

No cause for Jonathan's seizures has been found—no family inheritance factor, no unusual events during pregnancy and birth, and nothing at all preceding that first episode of 50 or more seizures within 4 days, with the exception of a runny nose and cough. There was no fever with that illness, and none of the CT scans or MRIs revealed anything that might suggest a cause. Medications—there are too many to name—were tried, alone and in combinations. The side effects were many and sometimes severe. We wondered then and we wonder now if the medications and their side effects are not worse than the seizures themselves. We do not know Jonathan without medication in his system. I cannot help wondering what my little boy would be like without anticonvulsant medications in his system.

Finding a way to stop Jonathan's seizures became a crusade for me. As a teacher, I was well aware that a child's brain is "set" by age 6. For me that meant finding a cure and arranging for therapy immediately, regardless of the cost in money, time, and effort—nothing else in life mattered, except helping Jonathan. As he grew older, the seizure episodes continued, all beginning with a sinus/upper respiratory infection, *without* fever, and usually ending with a hospital stay of at least a week, sometimes longer. I asked many questions of Jonathan's wonderful pediatric neurologist, and whatever questions he couldn't answer I asked of others. I contacted doctors and therapists all over the country, requesting information and studying the dissertations and studies they sent to me. I shared everything I learned with my family and friends.

The one person with whom I could not share was, of course, Jonathan. To this day his ability to comprehend abstract concepts and to correctly understand what he hears is significantly impaired. Many normal activities of everyday life are a struggle for him and, as his mother, I can only watch, pray, and try to be there to comfort him when the world is more cruel to him than I feel it should be.

I cannot write the word "pray" without some explanation. I am a strongly religious person with a grounded belief in Christianity, Jesus Christ, God, the Holy Bible, and the power of prayer and faith. I refused to accept Jonathan's seizures and the resulting brain impairments and developmental problems. I believed it could all be conquered and that I was the one to do it. There was a cure and I must find it. There was therapy and I must see that he receives it. The world could be cruel and I must defend him from it. Unfortunately, I placed too much responsibility on myself and my religion, and not on the God who is ultimately in control of everything. After 4 years I was on the verge of a complete mental and emotional breakdown. Twice I was hospitalized for major depression, the result of having thoroughly convinced myself that since I had failed, I needed to remove myself from the picture and let someone else try to do for Jonathan the things I could not. And yes, I made an attempt at suicide that I was certain would work. I was astounded when it did not.

I learned from the doctors, nurses, therapists, and counselors who worked with me during those long weeks and months that I had to let go of Jonathan. I had to stop blaming myself for every seizure that occurred, for every medicine that failed to work, and for limited finances that interfered with the treatments and therapy I was determined he should have. It was the hardest thing I have ever had to do, and even now it hurts deeply when I try to let go and let what will be, be. I no longer follow Jonathan to the bathroom every time he has to use the toilet for fear he will have a seizure, fall, and hurt himself. I no longer make him stay in the house so I can keep a close watch on him. I no longer forbid his participation in activities outside the home without one of us there to be with him. And I no longer make excuses for behavior problems I know he can control, for poor grades on tests when I know he did not try to learn the material, and for crying and whining when I know it is uncalled for.

Because there is no warning before Jonathan's seizures (he does not even know what a seizure is), seizures pose a great risk to him. Simply eating lunch in the school cafeteria with a fork in his hand can turn into a nightmare when a seizure starts, because he begins to uncontrollably move the fork around his face or near the person closest to him at the time. Just this year I was horrified to learn that Jonathan had disappeared from the view of his teacher and classmates only to be found sitting in the front seat of a strange car in the school's back parking lot. He was disoriented, sweating, very upset, and without speech—the usual pattern of his seizures. In the hour of postictal sleep after that seizure, I said over and over that I would never let him out of my sight again. The sense of horror at what could have happened is still with me, yet I have learned to let go once more, and I no longer leave my post as school librarian to "check" on Jonathan in his fourth grade classroom.

If nothing else, Jonathan's seizures have taught me what epilepsy is and what the families of disabled individuals go through for a lifetime. Never in my life had I seen a seizure of any kind, and I am ashamed to admit that I was once one of those people who thought of a seizure as a "fit of madness" and of the person as "mentally ill." Now I do all I can to correct that very wrong impression, not just for Jonathan but for all the children and adults who have to wake up every day knowing they could have a seizure in public. The sense of empathy I feel towards the families and care givers of all disabled people is strong and even overwhelming at times. I am sometimes intolerant of the behavior shown by some people towards a person who is obviously disabled.

The burdens are great for those who care for the physical, mental, emotional, social, and spiritual welfare of these special children and adults. Not only are there huge financial burdens and battles with health insurance companies, government welfare programs, hospitals, and collection agencies, but there are also burdens in being left out of the "normal" world. In our case, caring for Jonathan has been a 24-hour job, seven days a week, without any let-up. That is because very few people are willing to babysit a person with seizures; the legal ramifications if that person has a fatal seizure are too great for the average babysitter. It is possible to arrange for a registered nurse to sit with a child with epilepsy, but the expense makes it impossible for most families. It certainly did for us.

Someday I hope to develop a very personal ministry to the families and care givers of those with epilepsy and other profound disabilities. My husband and I have learned the value of a few hours out of the house and away from the disabled person. In my case, the constant care of Jonathan without any breaks proved to be too much and resulted in a disability of my own—major depression. Regardless of the lessons I learned and the strength and wisdom that came from my "dark" days, I still require daily medication. I probably will for the rest of my life.

I cannot close my story without adding that Jonathan himself seems to be better for my "letting go" of him and his epilepsy. He is developing confidence in himself and his ability to make the right decisions, and he has learned that there are other people just as trustworthy as his mother. He no longer cries hysterically when I "disappear" from sight, even if it is just from one room to another, nor do I have to escort him to his classroom every morning. It is such a joy for me in the mornings when I send him out the door of the library with a kiss on the cheek before school starts, knowing that he is satisfied to let go of me and begin to depend upon himself as he heads down the hallway to his classroom.

He now plays outside—alone—and does not mind if I am

busy preparing dinner. An occasional glance toward each other through the window satisfies us both. It means everything to me to know that Jonathan is no longer angry and afraid during his every waking moment. True, he has to deal with the occasional mean child who points, laughs, and teases behind the teacher's back, but that is life. That is the real world, and I prefer that he learn to adapt to that as he has learned to adapt to so many other things in so many other ways.

Jonathan's future might not be bright or happy. In fact, he might not even have a future. If the seizures themselves do not kill him, then whatever he is doing when he has one could. It is a definite comfort to me to know that he truly has the childlike faith of a believer in Jesus Christ. Although he is not eager for death itself, he tells anyone and everyone, with a surety that few Christians seem to have, that when he dies he will go to Heaven to be with Jesus. And that is enough for me.

20

(Age 9) I do not know what it feels like to have a seizure now because I'm always asleep when I have one. I sleep in my mom's bed because if I have a seizure I might fall out and bump my head. I used to have seizures in the daytime and I had to wear a helmet so that if I fell down my head would be okay. I fell down a lot. I knew I had a seizure because my mind would blank out. Afterward I would feel funny.

Sometimes kids treat me mean. They tease me because I can't have sugar, since I'm on the ketogenic diet. They say that I'm stupid. I'm *not* stupid: I'm smart! But they don't know how much the medicine that I take affects me. The teachers know that I am smart. They treat me like any other kid in the school.

I get tutored on Fridays to catch up in math because it's hard for me to concentrate when I do math at school. I play baseball and go to art classes just like a normal kid would do.

Having epilepsy makes my life hard, but I still go lots of places and do lots of things.

(Mother) Skyler's the youngest of our three kids and our only son. At $4\frac{1}{2}$, he was a typically rambunctious pre-schooler—bright, healthy, and normal in every way. After a relatively mild case of chicken pox he had returned to his Montessori school, where I'd lingered longer than normal before saying good-bye. He completed some work and was on his way to put the paper into his lunch box when his face froze in an odd grimace. I knew immediately something was wrong. When I got to him only steps away, he'd already stiffened and slumped to the ground, writhing and jerking. My thoughts at the time: convulsions, *my baby is in convulsions!*

Since then, Skyler's been through countless diagnostic tests, everything from CTs and MRIs and PET scans to metabolic and genetic workups. He's been on nearly every drug imaginable, alone and in combination. He's been in two clinical drug trials and he's been on antiseizure drugs obtained outside this country. He's been through "alternative" therapies as well, such as acupuncture, osteopathy, herbal remedies, chiropractic, iridology, reflexology, and hypnosis.

And yet he still has seizures every single day of his life.

We're lucky now, though. Ninety-nine percent of his seizure activity occurs when he's sleeping, so he's able to lead the semblance of a normal life. Once confined to soft surfaces for nearly 2 years, this personable, wise-cracking, fun-loving 9-year-old now attends regular school, plays Little League, attends art classes, and plays video games (much more than he should)!

Not to say his seizures haven't had an impact on his life . . . I could tell you about the short-term memory problems, and the gross and fine motor difficulties, the social ostracism, and so on, but that would be a great disservice to him. Because he's absolutely awesome. And he's still the same boy, even after all this. He's vivacious and tenacious and remains the bright and joyous soul he's always been.

We are 5 years into this hellish roller coaster ride known as intractable epilepsy. In the early days of Skyler's seizures, I prayed that this hideous nightmare would just go away altogether. When that didn't happen, I came to accept the epilepsy and just prayed that we could get the seizures under control. When that didn't happen, I learned to just take it one day at a time. But I've still not stopped praying.

He is my son, Skyler Flourie. I love him. And he is my hero.

21

(Age 12) This may sound really weird but I actually like having my blood drawn. It's cool to see my blood.

The thing I really hate though, is taking medicine. I have had to take it three times a day, seven days a week for 3 years! I think that's about 3,276 pills!

But maybe it's not so bad. I mean you get to skip school. *That's* worth it.

22

(Mother) Will was diagnosed with seizures at the age of 2. He never responded well to any of his medications. He continued to seizure several times a day and still had side effects from the medicine. Will's seizures, which lasted approximately 1

minute, began with right arm posturing. Then he turned his head and eyes to the right and lost awareness of his surroundings. He sometimes appeared to see things during the seizure. At the end of the seizure his arms and legs would stiffen. Afterward, he varied between continuing his activities or feeling tired and needing a rest.

Being so young, Will was unable to tell us how he felt before, during, and after a seizure. I came to realize he had an aura a few seconds before a seizure—he would call for me, seek me out and hold on, or kneel down. Now that Will is 5, he says that before a seizure he feels dizzy, has a headache, and feels as if he might fall.

Will had no developmental delays, so we enrolled him in a regular preschool for 2 years. We educated his teachers, who were very positive and responsive. Most of Will's friends and classmates were unaware of his seizure disorder. Our attitude about Will and his epilepsy was that he was a normal boy who happened to have seizures. We made every effort to make his life and our family life as normal as possible, talk openly about his epilepsy, and educate those who were part of his daily life. We are an active family—Will is the youngest of three brothers—and he had to learn to live with his seizures, as did we, and live a full life.

Will woke up one night last July seizing every few minutes. It took 6 days in the hospital for his seizures to stabilize. The neurologists said that Will had refractory seizures and that if he continued to seizure at this rate he would not grow up to be a normal boy. I remember sitting on the park bench outside the hospital wondering what would become of his life and ours. He was so little and living through a fog of medication. What kind of life was this? I can't say that we ever lost hope. We changed direction and went down that long road towards surgery.

Later on, Will was admitted to the hospital for LTM [Editor's note: long-term monitoring, see Glossary], which showed a definite focus in his left occipital lobe. The doctor was concerned that Will could lose vision if he had surgery. The neurologists and neurosurgeons believed that he was born with abnormal brain tissue in the left occipital lobe and that perhaps they could save some of his vision by pinpointing a smaller portion to be removed. As a result, they recommended that Will undergo invasive monitoring. As it turned out, the entire lobe had to be resected because seizure activity was found to involve most of the lobe.

Will had his occipital lobectomy several months later and has been seizure-free since. He will be off all medication a year from surgery. His current medication is greatly reduced, and he feels like a million bucks! He did lose peripheral vision in his right eye and all vision to the right through his left eye. But he has compensated for this loss almost completely and has not required any occupational therapy at this point. He began kindergarten this fall and is doing well.

Will doesn't talk much of his stays in the hospital, and if he does, he remembers things from a child's perspective—the red Jello-O, the Winnie-the-Pooh movies, the fun bed with remote control. I remember the same admission from a mother's perspective—the swollen, bandaged head, the painful seizures during invasive monitoring, the little boy who didn't move for 5 days. And the little boy who was so strong, stubborn, and courageous. His brothers who visited him were also brave and strong. Will made no friends among the doctors and nurses. He just wanted to get better and go home. Don't touch me, don't talk to me, "just leave me alone!" He's tough and aptly named—WILL!

Will has been seizure-free for 8 months now, and every day since his surgery we have been appreciative of how this has changed his life and the lives of everyone else in our family. And though most of the time we fully believe Will's seizures are gone for good, he can still posture his head at a certain angle, open his eyes wide with a certain stare, and I'll get the same punch-in-the-gut feeling as the first time he seized. That feeling is part of me, never to be forgotten.

Perhaps the people who had the most difficulty accepting Will's epilepsy were those closest to him, both sets of grandparents, and his brothers. When Will had a seizure, his brothers did what they had to do for Will's safety if I was not nearby, but as soon as I arrived they retreated as far away as possible and were clearly uncomfortable with his seizures. Both of Will's brothers have felt much anger and resentment towards Will, and towards my husband and me. The last 3 years have been difficult and demanding, from diagnosis through surgery, despite our struggle to keep things as normal as possible. Their feelings were normal and well-founded, and only now, 8 months after surgery, does it feel like that anger is fading away. Both sets of Will's grandparents live at a distance and were not witness to the daily challenges of living with a child with epilepsy. As a result when they were visiting us, they suddenly saw the reality of daily seizures, side effects of medication, and planning things a day at a time, perhaps even changing plans one moment to the next. Our family dynamics had changed, and that was difficult for them to adjust to.

We hope that Will is one of the very lucky children who can be completely cured of their refractory seizures through surgery. In all honesty, his prognosis is more than we dared hope for—we would have been thrilled with fewer seizures and less medication. He is a new boy. I like to think that all that noise from seizure activity is gone—it's quiet and peaceful inside his head now.

In my heart, there is finally peace as well.

23

❖ ❖ ❖ ❖ ❖

(Age 16)   How do I feel about my seizures? I feel embarrassed when I'm around a group of friends and have a seizure, because they are scared to see them. Sometimes I'll fake one and this is the reason they don't want to be around me. After I do that, they start calling me names and embarrass me.

Sometimes I'll have a seizure that only lasts 10 to 30 seconds—these are the ones that people think I fake. That doesn't make me feel right, because they don't believe me.

I feel jealous of other people who work because I don't have a full-time job. I need to make the money so I can put it in my bank account. But I have a reason why I can't work a full time job—there is a chance I might get hurt.

That is how I feel about my seizures.

24

(Mother) Like all parents we wanted the very best that life had to offer for our children. When our son was diagnosed with epilepsy, we were concerned but not overly so. Not knowing much about it, we assumed that medication would take care of the problem. We could not have been more wrong.

His seizures come on with an aura. When this happens he will say, "Oh, no" or "I'm having a seizure." He may talk during the beginning stages of a seizure, although he is rarely coherent. He will often say that he is sorry, but why he is sorry we do not know. His arms and legs will start to shake and his head deviates to the extreme left. His eyes and mouth will move rapidly. When the seizure is over, he is very tired, confused, and often has a headache. It can take him from 15 minutes to 2 hours to recover completely. If he is in school, he will have to re-learn everything he had been taught before the seizure.

We have been through every test, medication, and the best medical care available, with little or no success. When I say *we,* I know that the burden of these tests and drugs, not to mention the seizures themselves, is on our son's shoulders, but epilepsy is a problem that affects our whole family.

As we watch our son go through a seizure we can only imagine what *he* goes through. Not knowing can be as scary as knowing. Our fears are overwhelming and at times we have a tendency to overprotect him. Things that other children his age and younger can do without a care become a trial for us. Do we let him or not? Is it better to keep him safe or to let him live as any other 13-year-old? Every inch he gains in school is obtained with a great deal of effort on his part—nothing comes easy to him. His frustrations, anger, and fears are great, as are ours. "Why *our* son?" we often ask.

Guilt is mine all the time. What did I do to cause this? Why can't I make it better? What do you say when a child tells you all he wants for Christmas is to be seizure-free? How do you deal with children who don't like your child because he is "different"? Or with brothers and sisters who ask, "Is my brother going to die from a seizure?" I am sure that every parent of a child with epilepsy would like the answers to these questions, but no one has them.

Life is tough enough for kids these days without adding any other complications. Our job as parents is to make things as easy as possible for our children. Being parents of a child with epilepsy makes this somewhat difficult, but we will never give up or stop looking for answers.

We all have hopes and dreams for our children. With determination, strength, family support, and prayers, these hopes and dreams will be realized. We owe it to our son to allow him to live as normal a life as he can. We cannot and will not deny him.

25

❖ ❖ ❖ ❖ ❖

(Age 8)   My name is Julia and I am 8 years old. My mom and I are both epileptic. When I wake up, I sometimes feel like I

am going to have a seizure. My arms feel "z-z-z-z" tingly and I feel shaky inside. My head tips back and sometimes when I try to take my medicine, I spit instead of swallow. Mom puts a towel on my lap. She knows I want to swallow. I also take medicine at lunch and supper, but I do not have trouble swallowing them.

At breakfast time, I sometimes have trouble holding my milk. I have spilled the milk many times, but Mom doesn't get angry. She just asks me to lie down or wait a while before drinking more. Yesterday morning, I kept dropping my shoes. My hand wouldn't hold on to them. I took my medicine and waited a few minutes.

I do not usually have a BIG ("grandmother") seizure, especially if I rest. Mom asks me to lie down on my side so I won't fall if I have a big seizure. She will put a blanket on me or put me in bed if I can walk. I feel cold and my teeth knock together because it helps me to stay warm.

During a seizure my eyes blink very fast for a while and then I close my eyes and sleep. During and after seizures I have trouble talking. Sometimes I can't talk at all. Mom says this is part of the seizure and that my voice will always come back.

Two months ago I was watching a movie called "The Miracle Worker" on TV. It was about a girl named Helen Keller who couldn't hear or see. Her teacher taught her sign language so that Helen could talk with her fingers. I asked Mom to teach me sign language. I picked out an ABC book of finger spelling. When we had learned each letter, I practiced with my spelling words for school. Now, when I have a seizure and I can't talk for a few minutes, I can use my fingers to talk. It is also good to use finger spelling in places where I have to be quiet. It is better than whispering.

My mom doesn't have seizures any more, but she says she has to keep taking her medicine to stay that way. I have only been taking medicine for a year. My doctor is helping me not have "big" seizures by giving me medicine.

26

(Mother)   My name is Rhonda and my daughter, Morgan, is $2\frac{1}{2}$ years old. This is our story.

I was 25 when I found out that I was pregnant. I had a normal pregnancy except for a kidney stone that developed during my eighth month and which was watched closely by my OB/GYN and a urologist. I delivered Morgan vaginally (with forceps) the day before her due date. She had a huge bump on her right temple which was swollen. It was red and then purple, and finally bled under the skin until it eventually disappeared. However, she scored a 9 on her Apgar test and we were released from the hospital after 24 hours. We were told that everything was normal.

After about a week Morgan started "shaking" in her sleep. By this, I mean that her eyes seemed to vibrate in their sockets and turn to the right or left, and her head would follow the direction of her eyes. This would happen in the middle of a deep sleep and would last for about 30 to 45 seconds. It began happening 10 to 20 times a day. After watching this for about 3 days and asking for advice from family and friends, I took her to the pediatrician. He sent us directly to the hospital, where we were met by a doctor.

Morgan was put in a hospital room. I was told that every time she had a seizure episode I should push the red button and a nurse would come in. The problem was that every time I tried this the nurse would not come in for about 10 minutes, and by that time my daughter would be asleep. I now know that the period after a seizure is like a comatose state, during which she is very tired and sleepy. However, the nurses didn't realize this and so they thought that I was overreacting.

Over the next 8 days, my daughter had sixteen blood tests, three x-rays, five catheterizations for pure urine, and two reflux tests. Then I was told to take her home. I was told that she was fine and that I was a paranoid mother. The next day I videotaped Morgan having five seizures and asked my doctor if he could refer me to someone else. Another doctor agreed to see Morgan only for a diagnosis, with the understanding that I would return to a pediatric neurologist.

The new neurologist was watching my videotape when Morgan had a seizure in front of her. The doctor actually saw it and immediately prescribed medication and ordered an EEG. After that, Morgan was readmitted to the hospital and was put in a screening room with an EEG wired to her head and video cameras on her around the clock. The diagnosis of "infantile spasms" was made and she was kept on seizure medication. And I only had a week left of my 6-week maternity leave!

Soon she was discharged and was back under the care of her first neurologist. Now came the trouble of trying to find a daycare center to care for a child with seizures who was on medication. I finally had to leave her with a friend. I went about 6 weeks with my daughter on this terrible medicine when I finally went to the library. I saw all of the side effects of this drug and realized that my daughter was not progressing.

I called the doctor to set up another appointment. The nurse yelled at me and told me that the doctor should have been seeing Morgan every week for the first 3 to 4 months. I didn't know how she thought I could have known this, because the doctor hardly ever spoke to me. He was the one who had called me a paranoid mother, and I had a hard time being nice to him. No one ever told me to make a follow-up appointment.

When the doctor did see us again for Morgan's check-up, I asked him about other medications. I also asked him how to find out more about her diagnosis such as: If she outgrows this condition, what else might I expect, and what does infantile spasms turn into? What would happen when Morgan was an adult? I didn't think that a 30-year-old woman would have "infantile" spasms.

He basically told me to write my questions down and bring them in with me every week. I did this for the first 2 weeks, but he always answered my questions with "I don't know."

My mother-in-law had to take Morgan in for the third visit.

I couldn't go with them, because I had only been back to work for a couple of weeks and was taking off at least one day a week. My mother-in-law took my paper with all of my questions on it, and the doctor told her that if my daughter was not important enough to me for me to be there with her, then he did not want to see any of us anymore. Needless to say, we never went back!

I begged the other neurologist to take Morgan back. She has been seeing us ever since. She sat me down on my first visit and had me watch four videos which actually answered many of my questions. She did tell me that Morgan could outgrow infantile spasms, but that having seizures was not the full extent of her problems. Even if she did not have the seizures anymore, she would still be developmentally delayed. This was too hard for me to believe. The only sign I could see that anything was wrong with Morgan were these awful seizures. However, pretty soon she really began to fall behind.

The doctor suggested that I put Morgan in a more structured environment (meaning daycare). There was one place opening in my town. I signed her up, and we were the first ones enlisted. Morgan received physical and speech therapy there. It was great.

Now let's get to Morgan's seizures. Morgan's seizures started with small jerks of her head and jumping eyes. It was terrifying. After about 2 months they changed to harder jerking movements, pulling of her legs in toward her stomach and face contortions.

I just wanted the seizures to go away and have a normal child. I really believed that if we could stop the seizures she would be normal. We ran EEGs, MRIs, and other tests to see if we could find out why she was having these problems. The EEG did show a seizure pattern, but the MRI did not show any abnormalities. This is still one of the hardest things to deal with. We do not know why she has these problems. We cannot find any brain damage—however, there is obviously something wrong in her brain. We finally found a combination of medications that controls the seizures fairly well. One bad side effect of these medications is that she has bad mood swings.

She can go from a mild, happy 2-year-old to a child who does not want to be touched, loved, or spoken to.

One of Morgan's special quirks is that she is extremely sensitive to touch. She never likes to be touched on the head or have her hair brushed. She will not let you brush her teeth. She is still not eating table food because she has not learned how to chew. She is not crawling, walking, or talking. She does not even communicate with me in any way, except to clap her hands or cry.

Sometimes it is very frustrating and sometimes it's a challenge, but I cannot give up. I love her with all my heart and will never stop looking for a cure. If I were a scientist, I would only study disorders of the brain and try to cure my child. I will never have another child because I cannot be assured that he or she would be healthy. Financially, I could not afford another child with the same problems that Morgan has.

If I had one complaint during my $2\frac{1}{2}$ years of experience with seizure disorders and developmental delay, it is the trouble I had finding support. I found a program designed to teach parents of special children the laws regarding education for our children in the public school system. Through them, I learned of a program in my state that offers in-home support for children with hearing or vision problems. We have been receiving services from them for 2 weeks. Too bad I did not know about them 2 years ago. We only have 6 months left.

I am afraid about what will happen when Morgan turns 3 years old and I have to face public education. Her therapy will be cut in half and I am facing the challenge of having to send her to a school where I do not feel she will flourish. We just learned this week that it is time to get a wheelchair for Morgan. I cried for 2 days. My husband is so angry about it that he will not discuss it. My mother-in-law thinks that I am terrible for doing this to Morgan. It is not that I expect Morgan to grow out of her disabilities or even run and play like a normal child, but I am scared that once I put her in a wheelchair she will never come out. I know that it is up to me to get her the therapy she needs and work with her to encourage her to walk, but I view the wheelchair as a crutch and I hate to go out in public and get all of that sympathy. They do not know me or my child. I am so proud of all of the accomplishments she has made, and their pity or sympathy only seems to belittle what she has accomplished. It makes me angry.

Overall, I know that we still have a long road ahead of us. I know that Morgan will walk and talk one day even if she is not a radio personality or does not run a marathon (wouldn't that be great!). I don't think I could cope with everyday problems if I gave up hope. I just have to keep readjusting my expectations.

27

(Mother) My name is Lynda and my husband is Douglas. Our 8-year-old son Jeffrey was 3 when he had his first seizure. After having uncontrollable seizures for $1\frac{1}{2}$ years, Jeffrey was diagnosed with a rare brain disease called Rasmussen's encephalitis.

The first time Jeffrey had a seizure, I thought for sure he was dying in my arms. He was a normal, healthy 3-year-old who spiked a fever. One minute he was sleeping in my arms, the next minute his eyes rolled back in his head, he was frothing at the mouth, and his whole body was jerking out of control. Even though his eyes were open, he was unconscious and totally unaware of what was going on. Thankfully, my husband had some medical training and recognized that he was having a seizure. He laid him on the floor on his side until the ambulance arrived. Jeffrey seized for about 7 minutes. He was very tired and disoriented after it stopped.

As Jeffrey's disease progressed he had many different kinds of seizures. I was afraid to be alone with him for fear that he would seize and I would be helpless. I was obsessed with making sure he got proper rest. I drove myself crazy trying to figure out what was making him seize. Once I thought oranges were the problem. As crazy as it sounds I was glad to hear my son had a rare brain disease. At last we had a reason for the seizures and we had some options. It bothered us to give Jeffrey so many medications. The drugs just seemed to complicate things.

Jeffrey actually got good at knowing that he was about to have a seizure. He would feel the seizure coming and say, "I'm having one." His right side would twitch, but he would go right on talking and playing. His speech would slur and when it was over he would be sleepy.

Jeffrey had many seizures. Sometimes they would be as short as 2 seconds. His head would lunge forward and he would lose his balance. These seizures were frustrating because they were so short that nobody else ever saw him have them, so sometimes I thought *I* was going crazy!

I'm a firm believer that one of the best guides to diagnosing a child is the intuition of the parents. We knew long before the doctors did that we had a very sick child. With the help of a journal and a very caring doctor we were able to treat Jeffrey in his best interests.

When I ask Jeffrey what he remembers about having seizures, he says he can't remember anything. I'm not sure if he just chooses not to remember or if he really can't.

At age $4\frac{1}{2}$, Jeffrey had a left hemispherectomy to stop the disease and the seizures. It worked! Jeffrey has not had a seizure in 4 years! Although the surgery left Jeffrey paralyzed on his right side, he has managed to regain much use over the 4 years since surgery. He walks with a slight limp and wears a foot brace, but he walks and runs all day long! He lacks use of his right hand and probably always will. He has minor learning disabilities but does manage to stay in a regular second grade class with related services such as physical therapy, occupational therapy, and the resource room. His friends treat him great. The kids at school always ask him how his leg is doing. He rarely gets frustrated. He is a typical 8-year-old boy who loves whales, trains, and life.

My husband and I have never once thought that we made

the wrong decision regarding Jeffrey's radical brain surgery. After watching him seize day after day, 24 hours a day, we know in our hearts that we did what was best to give Jeffrey the best possible quality of life. Jeffrey was far more limited seizing with a whole brain than he is now with half of a brain that is seizure-free!

Jeffrey is truly a blessing.

28

(Mother)   Our daughter was diagnosed with infantile spasms at 8 months of age. The diagnosis changed the course of our lives forever, although we wouldn't come to realize that for some time. We simply didn't understand the scope of the words "seizure disorder" nor the far-reaching consequences that would follow. Now, $3\frac{1}{2}$ years later, we are more cynical and less optimistic. I guess that's just another side effect of dealing with more seizures on a daily basis for more than 3 years.

Having a child with a seizure disorder has affected almost every area of our lives. It has touched our educational activities, our social life, our emotional needs, our physical strength, and our financial resources.

Almost immediately after receiving the diagnosis, we bought a book with the hope of becoming more informed. We joined the Epilepsy Foundation of America. Now, we have a small library of books, pamphlets, EFA newsletters, and videos. We know more about seizures than we ever wanted to know, and even that is not enough. We have tried 10 different medications in various combinations without success. All of us suffered through 3 long, futile months on the ketogenic diet. We still watch our child seize over 100 times a day.

Our social life has also been affected by our daughter's sei-

zure disorder. Because of the increased risk of injury gener-
ated by her seizures, many adults are simply afraid to deal
with her, afraid she will be injured or afraid they will "do
the wrong thing." She requires constant supervision, special
seating, feeding assistance, special sleeping arrangements, and
diapering. She is dependent on her caregivers for all her needs.
We can't just drop her off anywhere for a few hours. Likewise,
a trip to Grandma's requires significant planning. Even going
out for dinner can be an ordeal as we gather food, cups, medicines, and portable chairs. Sometimes it's simply not worth
the effort. Taking her to someone else's home that is not
"childproof" is even more difficult.

Perhaps the most complex problems we have concern our
emotional needs, and the emotional needs of our extended
family. Everyone is concerned. They want to understand, they
want to help, but they live far away. So they ask questions,
which is fine to a point. Eventually, though, it's apparent that
they are questioning our efforts: Are we doing the right thing?
Are we doing enough? What if . . . ? Have you tried. . . ?
What about another doctor? It sure would help if they occasionally told us they feel we're doing a good job and they're
proud of how we are raising our child. Isn't that really more
important than the seizures? The seizures are one thing, and
granted it's a big thing, but there really is a lot more to our
lives and our parenting. Sometimes I wonder if they see that.

One thing we have learned through our struggles is that it
is very easy to feel alone and isolated. Nobody's situation is
like ours. There may be many similarities, but no one knows
exactly what it feels like to us. Yet we have found encouragement and support by talking with other parents about their
child's abilities and disabilities.

When our daughter was 18 months old we enrolled her in
an early intervention program. Without a doubt, this was the
best thing we could have done. In that program we were able
to laugh, cry, rejoice, and agonize with other parents in similar
situations. Professional therapists and educators encouraged
us, taught us, supported us, and cared for us. We learned about
available resources and ways to advocate for our daughter.

These dedicated professionals helped us with everything we needed concerning our child. Now that we have "graduated" from early intervention and are attending public preschool, we keep in touch with program personnel. More than anything else, the early intervention program helped us maintain our peace of mind and self-confidence at a time when we felt we had lost so much.

Caring for a child with seizures is very physically demanding. Our daughter craves intense physical activity. She jumps, bounces, climbs, and swings, all of which require some adult assistance to get started. She has to be lifted out of the bathtub and wrestled with to change her clothes. Because of her innate need for movement and stimulation, it is not unusual to find her hanging over the back of a couch or chair or bouncing on the cushions. This activity, coupled with her frequent seizure pattern, increases her chances of injury. For both of these reasons she must be supervised at all times.

One of the most difficult aspects of dealing with our daughter's seizure disorder has been her erratic sleep patterns. Medication side effects and nighttime seizures have combined to create many nights of interrupted sleep. One of our criteria for continuing any medication is how it affects her sleeping patterns. We need all the rest we can get.

Probably the most frustrating thing altogether is the financial impact involved. We frequently meet our insurance deductible in January each year. We continuously have to show that a service or a device is a "medical necessity." It is very expensive to have a seizure disorder. In addition to the "regular kid stuff," there are visits to the neurologist, medications, evaluations, and therapy appointments. There is the endless driving back and forth to these appointments. There is the time off from work for hospitalizations. One year we actually hit that magic number where the insurance pays 100% of all expenses—not really a cause for celebration. We make too much money to get any assistance from government programs but barely enough to pay all our medical bills. Keeping the finances in check can be very stressful.

Yet, everything is not measured by the level of difficulty.

There are plenty of good times mixed with the stressful times. Having a child with a disability has taught us to truly cherish the accomplishments that she makes. We have reevaluated our priorities and determined what is most important to us: that our daughter be happy, feel loved, and be able to participate in life as much as possible. Many things that once took a great deal of our time and energy are not even worthy of our attention now.

Many people have told us how much our daughter has touched their lives. They express their wish that they could take her seizures on themselves in order for her life to improve. They treat her like a regular kid while at the same time recognizing her special needs. We receive a tremendous amount of support from our friends.

We have learned to be more tolerant and open-minded towards those who are different. For all of us, it is our uniqueness that makes us special individuals. Some of the most "handicapped" people I know do not have a diagnosis. They are so-called "normal" people who are imprisoned by their own prejudices, their self-righteousness, and their lack of compassion.

Through all of our struggles, we have found comfort in the knowledge that there is always someone who is worse off than we are. Our daughter's condition is not life-threatening and she has never sustained a serious injury from her seizures. Her surgery was elective and wasn't essential to keep her alive. Thinking about these things helps us keep our problems in perspective.

Others in the community who don't deal with handicaps just don't understand. We don't want their sympathy. We are not special people. We have not been punished by God, and I'm not sure we've been specially selected by God, either. Rather, I think we are being molded into parents capable of caring for one of His precious children.

Our life would be very different if our daughter did not have seizures, but it wouldn't necessarily be better. Our child is a wonderfully cooperative, beautiful little girl. She captures the hearts of those she meets, from medical personnel to school personnel to church members. She has a sweet, undemanding, compliant disposition. She is not like other children, but we think she is the best! Even though many days we struggle just to get through the day safely, we are always thankful for our child, grateful to have her in our lives and appreciative of who she is.

Finally, "normal" is what you make of it. We don't focus on what our child can't do. We focus instead on who she is: a unique child, lovingly created just the way she is by the God of the universe.

Who are we to question His decisions and plans?

29

(Age 10)   I feel fine right before a seizure. Then after the seizure I have a bad headache and stomach ache. I have to lie down. I feel fine again in about an hour. Two times I got sick from my medicine and it took me a month to feel better.

My teachers are nice. They send me to the office if I have a headache. I lie down on a cot until I feel better. My mom tells the teachers about my seizures so they'll be able to tell if I have one in class.

The kids in my class are nice to me. Most kids ask what I have. I can do most things.

(Mother)   When my youngest child was 6 years old, she suddenly began to experience things so bizarre that she became anxious and depressed. Over the next 10 months I came to feel that the child I had known and loved no longer existed. I feared for her very survival and longed to have back the happy, carefree child she had been before the onset of her problems.

One day, my daughter came to me saying she had spinning

in her head. Then she began to have repeated sexual thoughts which caused her great distress. It became difficult to awaken her in the morning. She felt nauseated and had glassy eyes. She moved as if in slow motion.

Occasionally she reported having seen or heard things that she knew were not really there. Six weeks into this dark period, she asked me, "Why do I think I am losing part of my mind?" Several weeks after that, she calmly said, "Sometimes I wish I wasn't even born." When I asked what made her say that, she explained, "My head hurts so badly."

My husband and I had sought help for her the week the bizarre experiences began. None of the professionals caring for her agreed on a diagnosis. Therapists and psychiatrists caring for her sent us to neurologists, who sent us back to the mental health professionals. Each seemed to bring a different interpretation to test data. Among the various diagnoses considered were obsessive compulsive disorder, schizophrenia, sexual abuse, anxiety disorder, partial seizures, temporal lobe epilepsy, and migraine headaches.

Eight weeks into this distressing period, my child had an EEG. The test showed "wildly erratic" activity and she was put on antiseizure medication. At that point, I began to read widely on epilepsy and learned about different seizure types. I realized my daughter had probably been having seizures since the age of 3. Many times, as a very young child, she had come to me glassy eyed, complaining of a stomach ache. As I picked her up to comfort her, her heart would be pounding in her chest. She would have a temperature of about 99.6 degrees. I'd think she was getting sick, but she always got better within a few hours. I remember thinking she had quite an immune system to fight off infections before they could take hold. Little did I realize that these events were probably seizures.

Now, after her EEG, she continued to have this type of episode while taking the anticonvulsant, but the sexual thoughts ended. She did very well for about 8 months until she took an over-the-counter antihistamine and decongestant for about 3 days. The sexual thoughts returned, but they went away once we discontinued the cold medicine. It was at this point that I suddenly remembered that she was being treated for an upper respiratory infection when her bizarre experiences first began. She also was taking an antihistamine when her headaches were so severe she wished she hadn't been born. Needless to say, she no longer takes antihistamines or decongestants.

During the past 4 years I have observed things as my child slept that could have been the result of seizure activity. One night I sat in bed and read to her. I myself fell asleep and was awakened by one of her knees jerking into my back. She then began grinding her teeth, and finally she ran one of her hands up the middle of her nightgown. Suspecting I had witnessed a seizure, I stayed with her a while longer, and the exact same sequence was repeated as she slept.

This fall, I looked in on her one night before I went to bed. I saw her chewing over and over again. Then her knees shot up in a jolt. As I stood there watching, she returned to the chewing motion followed, once again, by a jolt that threw her knees way up off the mattress.

My daughter no longer takes the antiseizure medication because of its adverse side effects. She does take medication for migraines and is free of the severe headaches she once suffered. Her neurologist suspects that she will outgrow all of her problems. I hope he is right.

I am happy to say that my child, who is now $10\frac{1}{2}$ years old, leads an active life. She is pretty much the happy child I knew before the dark period entered her life and turned our world upside down. She is probably a more compassionate person for what she has been through.

I would rest better if we had even received a firm diagnosis. What she experienced when she was 6 years old was frightening beyond my powers of description. I take consolation knowing there are many sources for help should her severe problems recur.

TO CAROLINE
By: Her Mother

There is poetry in my soul,
And words that must be spoken,
Of an angel child encased in pain,
And a mother's heart that's broken.

Will we be free again
To live, enjoy, and be?
Will we ever understand
What caused such great anxiety?

How serious are her problems?
How distressful is her pain?
In the coming months and years,
will the child I knew come back again?

Or is she a new creation,
Different, yet still the same?
Will I shake off this sadness?
Will I cease to feel the shame . . .
of falling to pieces? of not understanding?
of needing to know? of being demanding?

Oh, Doctors, Doctors, you have been
Both my salvation and my bane.
Bear with me as I learn to ask questions
Without sounding blunt, panicked, or inane.

Suzanne and Daniel, please try to understand,
There is only so much of me.
When we get your sister stabilized,
I will focus on your needs.

Part II

To those who have helped us along the way,
We thank you for your kind support.
We've learned a lot; we're stronger now,
We're healing from the hurt . . .
of conflicting opinions and miscommunication,
of frightening symptoms, with no explanation.

With others struggling through stressful times,
We'd like to share what we have learned,
For help that's rendered graciously,
Should be graciously returned.

Four plus years have come and gone,
Our lives have settled down.
Good times outnumber the bad by far,
our gratitude abounds.

30

❖ ❖ ❖ ❖ ❖

(Parents) Our son Robert (whom we call Bobby) is now 12 years old. A couple of years ago, he was the Winning Kid in our state. Our other two sons, Joshua (age 11) and Zachary (age 8), also have epilepsy. We also have a daughter, Shana, who is 7, and we are lucky that she does not have any health problems.

As you can imagine, the boys have a lot of questions about why they have epilepsy and must take medicine and their sister doesn't. It's a question that we do not have any answers for. We are preparing to go for genetic testing, so maybe we will have some answers for them after that.

Bobby: Bobby was 10 months old when he had his first seizure. It was the most frightening thing that we had ever seen. Neither of us had ever seen one before, so we didn't have any idea what was happening to him. As we rushed him to the nearest emergency room 45 minutes away, we both wondered what was happening to our baby and when was it going to end. As we soon learned, this was only the beginning.

After the first seizure we were told that it was probably just a febrile seizure and that he would not have any more, and that if he did he would outgrow them, so not to worry. Sure they could tell us not to worry, they were not the ones living with him. Of course, this was just the first of many seizures. Yes, many of them did happen when Bobby was sick, but they also happened when he wasn't sick. It didn't take long before we realized that those doctors happened to be wrong in their predictions.

The only warning that Bobby had before a seizure was that he would say, "I feel funny." This usually was right before he would go into the seizure. They usually lasted about 3 to 5 minutes, but some of them did last a lot longer.

Once we realized that he was in a seizure, Bobby would

look gray, his body would be very stiff, and he would shake all over. It always seemed like a long time before the shaking would stop. His eyes would roll back in his head and his lips would turn a blue–gray color. I always felt helpless.

After the seizure he would be very tired and sleep for hours, and when he did wake up he would be very confused. It always seemed like a long time before Bobby would be oriented to what was going on around him.

Since Bobby has gotten older, he has started having more minor seizures. These are not as scary for us to see, but it is hard because he doesn't realize that he has had one and he is confused about what is going on. If he is watching a cartoon and he has a seizure, he misses something and has problems figuring out what is going on in his show.

We try to understand how he must feel, but we really can't, and that's hard for everyone. We can only imagine what it must be like to live with the possibility that a seizure could happen at any time.

For the most part, the kids in school have been very good to him about his seizures, but I know that it has helped that we have always been very open about the boys and their epilepsy. We have always let the boys know that their epilepsy is not something to hide, and that the more people who know about epilepsy, the better off everyone will be—the boys because they will be safer, and the other people because they will be prepared in case one of them does have a seizure.

Joshua: Joshua's seizures started when he was 13 months old. At the time, he was on an apnea monitor and we had a visiting nurse coming to our house to check on him. The nurse was at our house one day when she asked us how long had he been doing that. I asked her what she meant by "that" and she said something about Josh staring off into space. I said I called that "zoning out." He just seemed to be in a different place than the rest of us. He was so young that we didn't know what we were seeing. We knew that something was not right, we just didn't know what it was. We were so involved with him being on the apnea monitor and the possibility of the monitor going off because he stopped breathing, that I guess that we were just not looking for anything else. So we were surprised when Josh was also diagnosed with epilepsy soon after this.

When Josh has a seizure, he usually sits and stares. He sometimes will pick at his clothes or make chewing motions with his mouth. We really have no warning that he is going to have a seizure. We just have a "feeling" that something is not right. There is nothing that we can do during one, except sit back and watch and be ready to help when he comes out of it. There are times when we can have people over and Joshua has a seizure, and our company will not even realize that he has had one. They think that he is just acting strange.

Josh has it rough. He not only has epilepsy but he also has severe learning disabilities. It is very hard when you're only 11 years old and you are what Josh says is like being a freak. It's hard to make him understand that he is just like other people, especially when he feels so much different from other kids his own age. He has missed a lot of school because of one doctor's appointment or another, and this makes him feel different. He is also being treated for depression, which we feel has a lot to do with his difficulties in school. He is going to participate in Special Olympics this spring, so we are hoping that this will help him.

Josh will not talk about how other kids act towards him because of his epilepsy. He seems to be going through a stage where he doesn't want to talk about it at all, not even with us. I think he hopes that if he ignores it, then it will go away. I guess I can't blame him. I don't think that I would be happy if I had to consider taking medicine for the rest of my life.

We hope that he will come to realize that he is just like everyone else—it's just that he has seizures. We have never stopped our kids from trying anything that they wanted to do. I just hope that maybe Josh can get out of his slump, because he really is a great kid with a lot of potential.

We just need to convince *him*.

Zachary: Zachary was diagnosed with epilepsy one December. He also was diagnosed with learning disabilities at about this same time. He was $6\frac{1}{2}$, and we thought that he wasn't going to have the same health problems that the other boys have. We were wrong.

Zach had never really been sick, so all of a sudden he was just like his brothers. And he was scared. He had never been a real fan of going to the doctor's office, so the prospect of having to start taking medicine did not sit really well with Zach.

Zachary's seizures started out slowly, but in the past few months they have increased a lot. He has come home from school because of seizures more times than I can count. His teacher this year is excellent. She has a real knack for making him feel good about himself, even when he feels bad. The students in his room have been really good about his seizures. He has had a lot of them right in the classroom, and still none of the kids has ever teased him. He says that there are kids who sometimes tease him during recess, but he says he just ignores them.

Zach's seizures are usually mild, with staring and chewing being the most obvious signs that he is having one. His eyes are really red and he gets scared. He says that his stomach doesn't feel good and he seems to lose control over his body. Many times he ends up wetting his pants before the seizures are done. After the seizure, he falls almost immediately to sleep and he may sleep for 5 or 6 hours. After he wakes up he eats everything in sight. It's strange to watch him because he eats everything, even things that he normally would never eat.

One thing that we can tell you is that there are a lot of ignorant adults in this world, including some family members, who should know better. Since Zach had the seizure in February, some family members have decided that they do not want their boys around our sons, and this has been very hard on our boys.

We are just very lucky that not everyone has that attitude. I wish there was a way to show these negative people what they are doing to our sons, but it's almost impossible to change people who have no desire to change. So we do what we feel is best, which is to keep our sons away from these people as much as possible. Some people tell us that yes, we are doing the right thing, and others tell us that we are wrong, but, as with everything else, we have to do what we feel is best for the kids.

(Mother) Thank goodness for my husband Larry. He was always very strong and he dealt very well with the seizures. I always knew if I panicked he would be able to handle it. I don't panic anymore, but sometimes when one of the boys has seizures for a day or two, I am sure glad that Larry is nearby to take over when I have had all I can take, mentally as well as physically.

I know I don't have to tell you that having three kids with epilepsy is hard. But we feel that God does not give us anything more than He knows that we can handle. Yet there are times I think He has a lot more faith in us than we have in ourselves.

This is our story about living with epilepsy. I would like to thank you for allowing us to share our lives with you and we hope that something that we have shared with you will be of some help to you.

31

(Mother) My 6½-year-old daughter had her first seizure when she was 3 days old. At the beginning of this mini-seizure, she stiffened and then raised both arms while simultaneously exhibiting rapid eye blinking and lip smacking. The entire seizure lasted 30 seconds. I remember wondering how could a person blink their eyes so fast.

After unsuccessfully trying many seizure medications through the years, she has continued having daily seizures that vary in appearance, intensity, and duration (5 seconds to 45 seconds). On a "bad" day she has 100 seizures and on a "good" day, 20. Nothing in particular seems to trigger them. A general pattern is that the frequency and intensity seem to increase on trying to fall asleep at naptime and at bedtime. Her typical and most severe seizures show in the following ways. First there is usually eye rolling, then entire body stiffening and turning to one side or the other with one arm up and one down, legs scissored, face distorted, and breath holding. There may or may not be tongue thrusting or tongue/lip biting; sometimes she cries out at the end. Afterwards, she sometimes tried to sleep and/or she may cry for a few minutes, possibly from muscle aches. Many times she has a very frightened look on her face. Because of our child's very limited mental abilities, she is unable to communicate her feelings about her seizures to us.

The intense feelings of helplessness, frustration, and heartache have never gone away from watching our child have seizures. Because we believe that she, like every child, is on loan from God, we simply try to do our best each day at taking care of this precious charge by loving her and accepting her as our special angel. We pray that she doesn't experience any pain from the seizures. We also pray that, as we continue with her care in partnership with some wonderful medical professionals, research funds will continue to be made available so that an effective drug will one day be found to control her seizures.

32

(*Mother*) Having a child with epilepsy is a life-changing experience for everyone involved. Our daughter, Anna, started having seizures when she was 3 years old. She has several types of seizures. When she has the seizure that she has most frequently she always remains conscious. Sometimes she will cry during the seizure. I am almost certain that she is in pain.

She cannot talk or move at will, but she does understand what you are saying to her and is aware of the things that are going on around her. She also sometimes wets her pants.

When her seizures happen frequently, she has a terrible disposition, mostly towards me. I know that she must really feel bad. We try to go ahead with our lives and make Anna's life as normal as possible, but sometimes this is very difficult. We are very careful to make sure that she gets enough rest and that she doesn't get too hot in the summer.

Anna is in the second grade in a regular classroom with a full-time aide. The kids, as well as the teachers, are great with her. They fuss over who will push her wheelchair and who will help her with the other activities in her class. Several of the children have been with Anna since kindergarten and they are quite familiar with her seizures. They know what to watch for and what to do if she has a seizure, and it doesn't seem to make them uncomfortable. Sometimes her seizures will last up to 20 minutes, and this does cause them to ask a lot of questions.

Epilepsy affects our whole family, not just Anna. We also have a 12-year-old son, and it is not an easy task to be sure he participates in sporting activities and the other things that he is involved in. Our friends and family do not always feel comfortable watching Anna because they are afraid that they won't know what to do if she has a seizure. We do have a great support system with our family and friends, even though they don't always understand what is going on with Anna.

We are so lucky to have Anna in our family. She has taught us so much about life. She has been on many different types of medication, hospitalized several times for seizures, lost her ability to walk independently, and sometimes is even unable to sit unassisted. But still she NEVER gives up. She always tries her hardest to do what so many of us take for granted in our day-to-day lives. I feel that having Anna has made it harder for me to be a parent, a wife, a daughter, and a friend, but it has made me better at all of them because I appreciate life for what it really is each and every day. She brings so much joy to our family!

Thank you for giving me the opportunity to tell you about

our lives with Anna and her epilepsy. If this in some way will help or be a comfort to those of you dealing with the same problems, then it will be well worth my time.

33

❖ ❖ ❖ ❖ ❖

(Mother) My son says that "Having a seizure is like when you put the VCR on pause."

34

❖ ❖ ❖ ❖ ❖

(Age 12) Hi. My name is Luke. When I have a seizure I feel scared and I need to find my mom or dad. It feels like my heart stops beating and everything around me looks like it's shaking and blurry. Sometimes I can't talk. I feel like I am dying and I can't breathe. I don't want the kids at school to know I am having a seizure, so I turn away and cover my mouth so they cannot see my mouth twitching. The seizures that I have almost every day are hard for other people to notice. The kids at school don't know about them most of the time.

All my teachers are nice to me, but they usually don't know when I'm having seizures, except one time I had a very long one and could not talk and forgot where I was. My teacher took me to the nurse's office.

Because I have learning problems, some kids call me "retard," and now that I know what that means it makes me mad and sad.

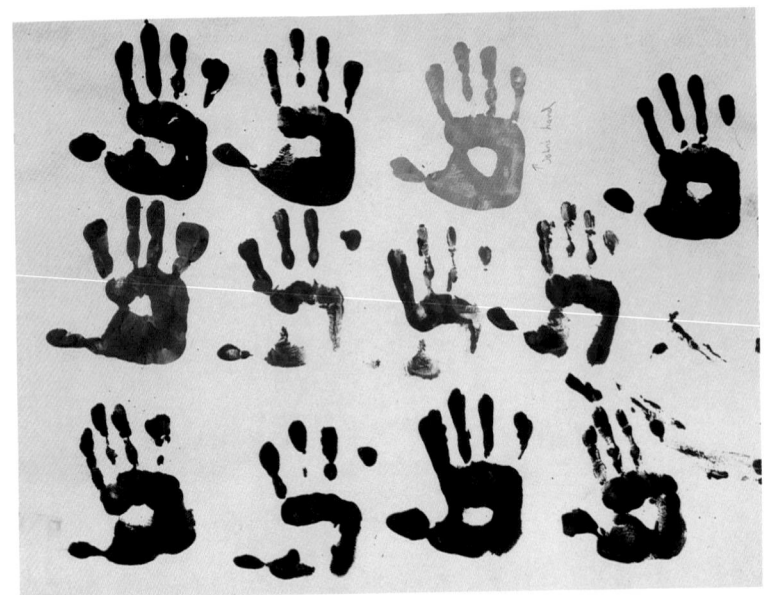

35

(Mother) My daughter was first diagnosed at 6 weeks of age. The diagnosis was infantile spasms. We really didn't know exactly what was going on with her until one day she started to blink her eyes and cry. She wouldn't stop. I rushed her over to her pediatrician's office. He told us what was going on with her. We were quite devastated and felt as if someone had pulled the life right out of us. With the proper treatment the infantile spasms stopped. But when she was 6 months old, she started having other types of seizures.

My daughter is 4 years old now and she continues to have seizures. Just before she has a seizure she will go into a blank stare. If it's only a minor seizure this will last about 30 seconds, and then she will tell me "I had a seizure" and go on with what she was doing before her seizure. After the blank stare she may go into a big seizure: she will fall, grind her teeth, and have some stiffening movements which will last about 30 to 40 seconds. After it's over she will gasp for breath, then begin breathing normally again and go directly to sleep for about an hour.

I think it is very important that we have a positive attitude about this, for ourselves as well as for her self-esteem. Over a period of time you learn to deal with it and try to give your child as normal a life as can be.

36

(Age 11) My name is Russell. I have a really hard time concentrating in school all day. I can do fine for a while, but then I lose my patience and can't concentrate. Then I get really angry with myself. I have even told people to just shoot me and get it over with.

It doesn't bother me to take medicine every day. That is just something I've been doing since I can remember. I know I'm tired every day, and when it gets too bad I take a nap.

Kids at school can be pretty mean at times. I've heard them say "don't go near him—you'll have a seizure." I'm lucky to have a little sister who sticks up for me!

My teachers help me with my seizures, but they still make me work too hard sometimes.

I can tell you that before a seizure sometimes I get this fuzzy or tingly feeling in my feet. All I remember about having a seizure is being out of breath. When one is over, I'm glad it's done and I am super tired and I go to sleep.

When I was having "drop attacks" I felt really clumsy. I thought everyone was looking at me. I also got hurt a lot. Once I fell into a barbed-wire fence and cut my forehead. Another time I fell on my sister's bike as I was walking by it and her kickstand scraped my whole side. That was painful. My knees were always scuffed up, and my hands hurt from falling on them, too.

If you ask me if I feel different from the other kids, the answer is yes and no. I feel like anyone else, but sometimes my head isn't clear and I feel like I can't do anything as well as anyone else can. I feel like I want to do something, but the brain power just isn't there.

Being the Winning Kid for a year was the best year of my life. I got to meet our governor. I dedicated books on epilepsy to our local library. I was the Master of Ceremony at a 50s and 60s dance for the Epilepsy Center. I judged a helmet awareness poster contest and gave speeches at school about my disorder. I also participated in Summer Stroll walks and helped raise money to go toward research for epilepsy.

I'd like people to know: *you can't catch epilepsy*. Everyone should learn more about it so that each person can be more supportive of people who have this disorder. I'm also hoping we find out more about what causes epilepsy and what we can do to make it easier for people like me who have it.

Epilepsy is something I just put up with every day—sort of like my little sister!

(*Mother*) One day in July, several years ago, Russell had his first seizure. He was 5 years old. We were all just waking up when I heard a strange grunting noise coming from his room. When I get in there, he was rigid. His arms were outstretched and jerking. His eyes were dilated and wide open. He wet himself and his eyes rolled back. I cradled him in my arms, not knowing what else to do. I soon discovered that was the wrong thing to do because he started to choke on his own saliva. His breathing was irregular and he was turning blue. He looked to me like he was dying.

I was in total panic. My husband and I rushed Russell to the clinic to have our doctor look at him. By the time we got there (I can't tell you how long this first seizure was because when you don't know what's going on, you don't time them) Russell was back to us. He could look around, talk, and even crack a few jokes. But when the doctor examined Russell, he had Russell try to raise his arm—Russell couldn't. The doctor asked him to tap his forefinger and thumb together—he couldn't. Russell could follow the doctor's finger with his eyes, but was feeling really sick. Within minutes Russell said he wanted to sleep. He slept, all right. Five hours went by before he awoke. When he did wake up, he threw up quite a few times because I had held him the wrong way while he was in the seizure. I didn't know I should have rolled him on his side so he wouldn't have choked. I think that, as a Mom, I had as rough a day as Russell did.

After Russell had blood drawn and had an EEG and a CT scan, the doctor concluded that Russell had a benign form of epilepsy, and he sent us to a specialist. Russell was put on medication. As little as we knew of this medication—we prayed for it to "fix" him. Russell had no seizures for a year, so we decided to take him off his medications. But after we very slowly stopped the medication, Russell had more seizures. He was then put back on medication and was seizure-free for another year.

Then another nightmare began. Russell was having seizures every 2 weeks! This lasted for the next 2 years. Up until this time, Russell always had his seizures right as he was waking and while he was in bed. Then they started changing. He started experiencing drop attacks. He'd stumble, fall down, look drunk, and be confused during the day. His left side was affected the most.

I started videotaping Russell during these episodes. I've been keeping a daily calendar since the first seizure he had. I know better than anyone how he acts when he's going to have a seizure or a drop attack. I also know when he just needs to lie down and go to sleep.

It is nearly 6 years later now and Russell is on a new medication. His seizures are very controlled, but his moods are excessive. He's high or really low, angry one moment and weepy the next. We've tried extra vitamins, changed his diet a hundred times, had him on two medications at once, and even had him take his medication at certain times for more structure.

I have to admit that the seizures don't scare me anymore. I know Russell won't die and he won't have brain damage, but just when I feel confident about it all, he'll have a super bad seizure and I turn to Jello again after he comes out of it.

I talk to Russell while he's in a seizure. He is usually looking directly at me as if he is trying to talk. His eyes have an accusing look most of the time, as if to say, "Did you forget to give me my medication?"

The last huge seizure he had was 10 full minutes long. I don't think I can explain the sick, empty, helpless feeling I have while he is in a big seizure. Once I cried hot tears of fear and anger because I couldn't get through to Russell. His eyes were totally unresponsive and dead looking. They were fully dilated. His jerking was worse than I'd ever seen, and my cooing, soft voice, and petting did nothing to calm him down. So I started yelling. I screamed, "Fight it Buddy—don't let it get you—you're stronger! It can't win—you can do it—you're the only one who can beat this thing—don't let it win!" It was odd, but he seemed to respond to that. I could see him giving it his all to fight back. I could feel him gaining more and more control.

Russell's a very strong boy and I admire him so very much, but a part of me has to wonder just what kind of boy he'd be without the effects of the medication. Is he who he really is, or is he what the medications make him?

Here are the things that I can recommend to you, things that have helped me as a mom with a child with epilepsy:

1. Keep a daily calendar. Someone will learn more about the disorder by collecting information about how it affects each individual.
2. See a neurologist. We've been lucky with ours.
3. Join a support group, not only for your child but for you.
4. Read everything you can get your hands on about epilepsy. I have given speeches and joined a parent network, which is good for parents who can talk on the phone but are too busy to meet.
5. Watch and love your child. Don't stop him or her from living—rather, help enhance his or her life for as long as you can.

37

(Mother) As a parent, I felt devastated when I learned that Melanie, my daughter, had a seizure. I was not with her during her first seizure. It happened during preschool toward the end of the day. My neighbor was at school to pick up Melanie and her own son. She called me and said, "Melanie's having a seizure! They're calling an ambulance." I dropped the phone and took off. Thank God I had a car. I got to school and found her in the ambulance, unconscious.

I was really scared. I never knew anyone with epilepsy or anyone that had ever had a seizure. At the hospital I learned that there are many reasons for seizures, including brain tumors and serious viruses. After 2 days of tests they told me that Melanie did not have a brain tumor or encephalitis but that her EEG was abnormal, so they diagnosed a "seizure disorder" or epilepsy.

In those early days I was overwhelmed with questions. Why would a healthy 4-year-old suddenly develop epilepsy? Would she be able to go to a regular school? Would she have a normal life? I knew absolutely nothing about epilepsy then.

I immediately called the Epilepsy Association and got all of the information that they had. I guess I was relieved to find out that epilepsy can often be brought under control with medication. I hoped that Melanie would be one of the lucky ones that would have her seizures controlled.

Now, 9 years later, I feel that we *are* very lucky. Melanie is 13 years old and, although she still takes medication every day, she has not had a seizure in almost 4 years. We are going to get a new EEG to see if we can wean her off her medication.

Melanie definitely lives a normal life. She does well in school and has a well-rounded social life. She participates in sports, clubs, acting, and dance. I remember, when she was younger and she wanted to spend the night at a friend's house, I hated to let her go but I did because I didn't want to overprotect her. However, I was up all night with a sick feeling in my stomach, wondering if she took her pill.

These days I don't worry as much and I am very confident that she will outgrow her condition. Even if she doesn't, I know that she will take her epilepsy in stride and not let it interfere with anything she sets her mind to do.

38

(*Mother*)   When my son was born, he was a healthy newborn weighing 7 pounds and 3 ounces. His seizures began when he was 6 months old. Over the years, he has experienced several different types of seizures. Sometimes the attacks will give a warning. When this occurs, he may suddenly cease his activity, run to me, appear dazed and confused, and scream out as if he is afraid of something, or he may simply say, "I'm cold!" Then, I lay him down to make sure he is safe. Usually his entire body stiffens, his arms flex, and his legs, head, and neck extend. At the same time, his jaws clamp shut, and then a violent jerking movement takes over his body. The sound of air forced through his mouth is enough to scare anyone to death. The attack ends after about 60 seconds or less (but seeming more like forever), and the movements become less intense and finally cease entirely. At the very end of the attack, he foams at the mouth and sometimes urinates. When he wakes up from a deep, but short, sleep after the seizure, he is fully conscious but usually feels tired and sleepy. I always talk to him to let him know that I am with him and that he is all right. Then I put him to bed and he sleeps for several hours more.

The seizure I just described was pretty scary, and my son has had many like that one since then. But nothing compares to his first seizure. It was the morning he died in my arms 14 years ago. It was horrifying, and I still have nightmares about it. The night before, he was irritable and not feeling well, so I put him in bed with me. About 6:00 A.M. he woke up jumping in his sleep. A few minutes later, it seemed like a mighty force raised him into a sitting position. I reached to pick him up and he began this terrible, ear-piercing scream. All of a sudden his head went back, his neck and back arched, and his body became stiff. There was so much power in his little body that I could barely hold on to him. Quickly, I began to pull on my clothes and run with him still in an arched position to the car. His skin was turning darker.

About halfway to the hospital, his whole body began to turn a darker blue but he was white around the lips. He began making sounds like an animal. Then, suddenly, he became limp in my arms. There was no movement and he was not breathing. My husband yelled at me to start mouth-to-mouth resuscitation. I covered his mouth and nose with my mouth.

After about three breaths he began coughing and breathing again.

After many tests in the hospital, he was diagnosed with a seizure disorder and was placed on seizure medication. After that, and for a very long time, I ran with him to the hospital each time he had a seizure. By the time he was 3 years old, I was a physical and emotional wreck trying to cope, because despite his medication, his seizures remained uncontrolled. Yet his doctor worked very hard to do everything possible to help him.

Since then, he has gone from having many seizures every day to five or more a month to the present: he has been seizure-free for 5 months.

Our son is very special to us and we love him dearly. Our family has come a very long way. Now we are better able to help him and to deal with his condition. When someone asks how in the world are we handling this situation, I tell them "with the grace of the Lord and a very wonderful doctor."

39

❖ ❖ ❖ ❖ ❖

(Parents)

Pre Seizure: Sarah, now in second grade, will frequently rock back and forth and almost seems to hypnotize herself. The rocking usually lasts 1 to 5 minutes. During this time Sarah's eyes are usually fixed on one object.

During Seizures: Sarah will stop, stare, and be totally unaware of her environment. She will not respond to voices or visual stimulation during this time. This usually lasts 30 to 90 seconds. If Sarah does not have an aura, then whether she is reading, doing homework, or whatever, she just suddenly becomes disoriented and stares.

After Seizures: Sarah is usually very tired or lethargic, and usually naps. At school she may struggle with work that she was able to accomplish before the seizure.

Her First Seizure: Sarah had her first seizure 2 months before her second birthday. She was in the back seat of the car in her car seat. We were driving along and singing songs when she suddenly let out a high-pitched screech. I looked in the rear view mirror in horror. There was my princess—stiff as a board, eyes rolled back, and her body arched!

I felt frozen in time. It seemed like hours until I was able to pull to the side of the road and get out of the car, though in reality it was only a few seconds. Sarah was still stiff and she was drooling. She made no sounds at all and did not respond when I called her. As I pried her out of the seat, I kept thinking: What is happening? How could my beautiful, happy, healthy girl turn into this distorted being?

As time passed and tears flowed, I gained some inner support and realized I was close to the pediatrician. I put Sarah in the front seat and drove the short distance to the doctor's office. Sarah was limp by the time we arrived and totally asleep. This was the first time I heard that horrible word "SEIZURE."

Now when Sarah has a seizure, I still get a knot in the pit of my stomach but I know that the best thing I can do for her is to stay calm, keep her safe from her surroundings, and be reassuring when she comes out of it.

We have had mixed reactions from children and teachers. When Sarah first started kindergarten, she had many seizures and could often be found asleep somewhere in the classroom. This became a problem because parents were telling us and the teacher that if only Sarah would go to bed early, she would not have to sleep in school. Kids were beginning to stay away from her for fear of catching what she had. By January it was so bad that the teacher sent a letter to all parents sharing the fact that Sarah had epilepsy and it wasn't just a matter of her not getting enough sleep. This helped, but through her first year of school, Sarah had not really bonded to anyone in her class.

When Sarah entered first grade an aide was assigned to her.

The social skills of the class still left a lot to be desired, and we had many meetings in the early part of the year to find ways of creating social bonds between Sarah and her classmates. The problems intensified as other children moved on academically, while Sarah was falling further behind. Some of the children began calling her names and ridiculing her to the point that she dreaded going to school. Her seizures seemed to lessen but we felt that the aide was not aware of her seizure activity. She spent many days in the nurse's office, sleeping.

Sarah joined the Brownies but was not well accepted and missed many meetings due to post-seizure naps. Sarah received resource room instruction, and the special education teacher had a very difficult time understanding her mood shifts. She felt that Sarah was playing games or being defiant when she could not respond appropriately. This was a very trying year, and Sarah repeated first grade.

Repeating first grade did not go well for Sarah. She remained with the same teacher and aide. Socializing was still a class struggle, and Sarah had a difficult time making friends. Academically she made some gains, but was still behind the other children. Seizure activity seemed to decrease but, again, we weren't sure it was less activity or failure of the school personnel to spot the activity. Once again, Sarah had a very difficult time with her special education teacher.

Sarah is now in the second grade and has made some huge gains. I feel that this is in large part due to her current teacher and aide. They are both warm, caring, loving people who have made it a personal challenge to see that Sarah succeeds both academically and socially. This year Sarah has learned to read, and through innovative teaching techniques, she has done well in math and spelling. The change in teacher and aide has made her feel very important and she has responded positively. The other day she told us that no matter how old she gets she will always find time to come back and visit her current teacher and aide. I think the biggest change in Sarah's development this year is that the classroom teacher has taken full charge of her program and has the special education teacher working with her, whereas in the past, the classroom teacher keyed off the special education teacher. Sarah has also developed some strong friendships this year and speaks freely about having a best friend. She is well received by her classmates and an integral part of the classroom activity.

I hope that you will find this information helpful.

40

(Age 8) Before I have a seizure, I will usually experience an aura. An aura is something that warns you before you have a seizure. My auras only last about 5 seconds. I have a funny sour smell or an upset stomach or headache. Or I get dizzy.

My auras are too short for me to do anything about the seizure that follows. Sometimes I have only auras. One of my doctors told me that my auras are actually small seizures.

During a big seizure everything goes black and then I see things that move really fast. It's kind of like watching a video in fast forward. I don't like this feeling. I don't have any idea of what my body is doing and I don't feel any pain. I may have an accident.

During other seizures, I am aware of what I am doing. Usually my right arm, hand, and fingers start to wiggle and shake. I can't stop them from shaking.

After another type of seizure I am very confused. I don't know where I am or have any idea of what happened. It's kind of like a dream. I also am scared and very tired. I need someone with me.

My friends and the other kids don't really treat me any differently from other kids. In my new school I am not sure if all the kids know that I have epilepsy. But the friends that do know just ask a lot of questions, like, what do you do when you have a seizure?

My teachers really don't treat me any differently either. I

don't think they really know that much about epilepsy. My mom will come in and teach them if they want. One of my teachers asked me if I would be willing to talk to another kid in my class who just found out that he had epilepsy. I said yes. My soccer coach doesn't treat me any different either. I am not sure if she knows.

I am lucky because none of the kids in my new school have ever seen me have a seizure. I think if these people would ever see me have a seizure, they would probably be scared and judge me differently.

(Parents)

Seizure Type A: Usually no warning/aura. Aware but unable to control his physical movements. Usually has twitching of right hand, fingers, arm. Twitching stops and he experiences mild confusion. During a febrile illness, he experienced many seizures in which his right hand would repeatedly posture. He was aware of what was happening but he was unable to control his/fingers.

Seizure Type B: Usually experiences an aura. Will say that he smells something funny or strange which no one else can smell. Has a headache or says that he is "dizzy." Approximately 1 to 5 minutes later, he will stare blankly ahead, does not blink or respond to sound or touch. Usually right hand, arm, fingers twitch or tremble. Occasionally has raised right arm as if wanting the teacher to call on him to answer a questions, or some other repetitive motion, such as walking to the pencil sharpener and then back to his desk and repeating this again. Twitching or automatic behavior ends after usually 1 to 2 minutes. Blank stare ends with blinking and awareness of his surroundings. Confusion that ranges from mild to moderate may last for several minutes to several hours, and mild fatigue follows.

Seizure Type C: By far, this is the most frightening of all the types of seizures that a parent (or anyone) can witness. This is what most people envision when they think of seizure/epilepsy. Usually, he has an aura, same as above, then makes a moaning sound followed by his back arching and eyes rolling up into head. Whole body stiffens, arms are bent at the elbows, hands clenched (or clawed as Aaron calls it) and placed very close to his chest. Aaron falls solidly to the ground, much the same as a wood board would if stood on end and the top was let go. Breathing is very shallow or nonexistent, lips usually turn blue, and he may have a slight amount of bubbly saliva coming out of the corner of his mouth. This stage lasts about 30 seconds and then his arms and hands begin to quiver. The quivering stops. Aaron takes an enormous breath in, eyes return to normal, and he blinks several times. Marked confusion and fatigue that lasts for several hours afterward. (How many 8-year-old children do you know that would sleep for 3 hours on Christmas day!) He is unable to relate what happened and is unaware of any injury he may have sustained during the fall or seizure.

How did we feel the first time we saw Aaron have a seizure? As we sit here and think about this question, the emotions and feelings we experienced while watching our son have his first seizure are as real and consuming as they were $3\frac{1}{2}$ years ago. It is something that we will never, ever forget.

The fact we had no forewarning of his first seizure, and that it happened on Christmas day, intensified our feelings of shock, disbelief, and terror. We were not sure whether our son was alive or dead for what seemed then like eternity to us. What was happening? Why can't we stop this? We are his parents. We are supposed to be able to comfort him and make it better. But all we could do was watch him, helpless.

This single event was one of the most horrifying scenes we could ever witness. From the second he was born and we knew that there was a life we had created, an extraordinary never-ending bond was present. From that moment on we began to cultivate hopes, dreams and goals for our child. We envisioned birthdays, Christmas gatherings, graduations, weddings, band concerts, sporting events, and the births of our grandchildren.

All of that was swept away from us in those minutes in our kitchen. We were left with an immense feeling of loss, loss for our son's future and for our dreams of our future together.

When the diagnosis came and we knew the name of this unwelcomed visitor, and that it would be with us for a while, enormous guilt filled in the cracks between the loss. What had we done that would make our son suffer seizures? What medicine had we given him that caused this? We must be horrible parents, why else would *our* son be the one to have epilepsy?

How does it feel to see our son have a seizure now? A lot of the same feelings felt on that Christmas day come back even now when Aaron has a seizure. We still feel grief and a sense of helplessness. But it isn't as intense as $3\frac{1}{2}$ years ago. We have learned that there isn't an answer to the "Why Aaron?" And we still have a hope that his seizures will end as suddenly as they came.

Yes, we still wish that we had the super power of parents and could make his epilepsy go away. But we have also accepted that we don't have that power. We are still afraid of what discrimination Aaron may have to endure throughout his life. And we worry about the effect that will have on him. We have educated ourselves intensely, and for us knowledge is power. We know what epilepsy is and, more importantly, what it is not. This education and time is the most important step that you as a parent of a child with epilepsy can take, not only for your sake but also for the sake of your child.

(*Sister*) The first seizure my brother Aaron had was on Christmas day 3 years ago. He was playing his new electric guitar and he poked his finger on one of the strings. He came out of his room and said that he felt kind of dizzy. The next thing we knew, he was on the kitchen floor.

At first, we thought he was just faking, but after a few seconds he was still lying on the floor, so then my mom turned him over and his eyes were rolled up in his head. My dad finally called 911.

I thought Aaron was dead.

My brother was awake before the ambulance arrived. His nose was bleeding but it wasn't broken. I was glad my brother wasn't dead. One of the men that came in the ambulance said that Aaron had fainted, which was wrong. Later a neurologist said that he had a seizure. That's how I found out my brother had epilepsy.

Now I know how it feels to have a family member that has epilepsy. I'm happy I can help my brother.

41

(Age 9) My name is Merri and I am 9 years old. I have seizures. I take medicine every morning and night. My seizures would be very difficult at school if my teacher did not know about seizures. Since she does, the other children also understand me. Sometimes my teacher lets me take my spelling test over again if I have had too many seizures.

Someday I hope the seizures will stop. My family and friends pray about that every day.

42

(Father) My son, Chris, was diagnosed as having epilepsy four years ago. The diagnostic period was approximately 3 months and began after Chris had what *we* thought was his first seizure, at home and soon after bedtime. He had another seizure several months later, just a day before he began taking medication in an attempt to control his seizures.

Before these two seizures, Chris had no history, to the best of our knowledge, of any seizure activity. The first seizure happened after a head injury. Here's what happened.

Chris apparently slipped on a pencil in his classroom, fell down, and bumped his head. The school nurse was called to his classroom, and she subsequently reported that his eyes were rolled back, and she thought that he had some type of a convulsion. An ambulance was called and Chris was taken to the emergency room. After the attending doctor performed a battery of tests, he made the diagnosis of a mild concussion. Any symptoms that Chris displayed after he fell were attributed to the head injury. We accepted this diagnosis without hesitation, only to learn about 6 months later that his fall in school was in fact due to the seizure, not to slipping on a pencil.

Just before Chris went into that seizure, he was attempting to get the teacher's attention by raising his hand to tell her he had a funny, numb feeling in his thumb. Since he did not get a response from his teacher, he got out of his chair to approach her desk so that he could tell her about this funny sensation. Before he got to the teacher's desk, Chris went into the seizure. I do not think he was able to convey this part of the story to the doctors and nurses in the emergency room. From what I remember, Chris was not asked any questions that would have prompted this information. And everything taking place in the emergency room that day was centered around the possibility that he slipped on a pencil, fell to the floor, and bumped his head, not that a seizure was the actual problem.

During the diagnostic period, Chris was asked many questions about his memories of the seizure and he mentioned the tingling feeling he had felt in his thumb right before having the seizure. He also mentioned that he was trying to get his teacher's attention right before he had the seizure.

My wife and I have not witnessed any of Chris's other seizures, but our older daughter, Irene, has. She was 3 years old when she first saw Chris have a seizure. She saw him shaking on one side of his body and his eyes rolling. Then she saw Chris fall off the bed. She was scared and immediately realized something was wrong. She ran downstairs to tell us and we ran upstairs to find him on the floor and slouched up against the wall. He looked extremely weak. His body felt clammy, his heart was racing, and the top part of his tee-shirt was very wet from saliva that he had drooled during the seizure. We took Chris to the emergency room. We knew something was definitely wrong. This began the diagnostic period.

The other seizure that our daughter witnessed was several months later. On this particular night, as young children sometimes do, Irene and Chris were asleep for the night in the same bed, Chris's bed. I guess it was Irene's turn to sneak in Chris's room.

Anyway, soon after they fell asleep, Irene was abruptly awakened by Chris. At first, Irene thought Chris was bumping into her on purpose. She told him to stop. He wouldn't. She told him to stop again. Again, there was no response. At this point, Irene saw a lot of saliva and drool coming from Chris's mouth. She pleaded with him to stop fooling around, but quickly realized that something was wrong. This is when she ran to our bedroom for help. Irene's adrenaline was pumping. She told us to hurry up because something was wrong with Chris. I got to his room to find him on the floor ''sitting'' slouched up against the bed. From what I had learned during the previous 3 months, I knew right away that Chris had just had a seizure. Again, he was very weak but conscious. His skin was clammy and heart was racing. As was the case after his second seizure, the top half of his tee-shirt was very wet from saliva that he had drooled during the seizure.

Our course of action after this seizure was quite different compared to the first one that he had at home, because we had learned a lot since then. So although finding Chris in this condition was somewhat unnerving, it only took us a few minutes to focus on the situation and make the appropriate decision. That decision was to help Chris back into bed after getting him a drink of water and reassure him to the best of our ability. I knew that a call to our doctor could wait until the morning. And, it just so happened that Chris had a doctor's appointment the next morning to discuss his diagnosis. The purpose of that appointment was also for us to let the doctor know what course of action we would take in terms of whether or not to begin medication in an attempt to control Chris's seizures.

Our decision that next day to accept the doctor's recommendation to begin seizure medication was not that difficult, but there definitely was some initial hesitation. And, from the first time we were with Chris right after his first seizure to the present day, we've experienced many different feelings as a family. Regardless of the different feelings that we've had, coming to accept the fact that Chris was diagnosed as having epilepsy, and being as positive as possible, were the keys.

As things have turned out, Chris has not had any seizures since starting seizure medication. It appears that the medication has worked very well to control his seizures. Of course we were concerned about possible side effects of the medication, but the fact that his seizures were controlled seemed to outweigh this concern, and, as it turned out, there were no noticeable side effects. Chris was very responsible when it was time to take his medication. His doctor began to wean him off of his medication last year, and about a year ago he took his last dose. At that time we were told that the first 6 months would be the biggest hurdle in terms of possible seizure activity. As far as we know, Chris did not have a seizure during that period. Well, it has now been a year and 2 weeks since Chris has been off of medication and to our knowledge he has not had a seizure.

His school work has been good and he continues to participate in various activities. He rides his bicycle (with a helmet) to school every day, he has his own paper route, and he participates in gymnastics. To be quite honest, when Chris was diagnosed, not too many changes were made concerning his activities. Of course, we discouraged any tree climbing, made sure that he wore a helmet while roller skating or bike riding, and took necessary precautions when he went swimming. Also, his principal, teachers, and friends have been very supportive, understanding, and sensitive when needed. Open communication concerning Chris and his seizure disorder has helped to foster these attitudes.

Even with the progress that Chris has made, there is still a feeling of caution. I suppose that if the EEG that Chris was given just before the "weaning" process began was normal, I might proclaim that Chris no longer had epilepsy. However, that was not the case, so we try to keep things in perspective.

We continue to keep in touch with our local Epilepsy Foundation, which was instrumental in providing the support we needed when Chris was diagnosed. Many good things have happened from that simple call we made to our local Epilepsy Foundation in search of some answers and support, and we try to give back to them by helping out in various ways. Also, from our experience we've been able to help educate other people concerning epilepsy and seizure disorders. Recently, a friend's son was diagnosed with epilepsy. We've been able to provide some support to them, which makes us feel good.

So, even with something that initially seemed scary and raised many questions, accepting Chris's diagnosis enabled us to continue to lead a very normal lifestyle. Acceptance is very important because this ultimately affects what happens in the future. As I've mentioned, our association with the Epilepsy Foundation has led to some really neat and rewarding experiences. I suppose this chapter in our life will never be closed, as there will always be some epilepsy-related challenge to help with.

As I begin to close, let me share a quote from my son, Chris, "I think kids with epilepsy are Winning Kids because they are special. Even though they may have seizures, they can still do most things that other people can do. To do this, it is important for kids with epilepsy to take their medicine every day. Also, kids with epilepsy have many friends. These are the reasons that kids with epilepsy are Winning Kids."

As you can probably tell, Chris has had many positive and rewarding experiences in terms of dealing with epilepsy. I think that this has helped him and our family immensely. I hope this information has helped other people as well.

43

❖ ❖ ❖ ❖ ❖

(Age 12)   The way I feel when I have my seizures is awful. I go blind for about 45 seconds. I feel like my eyes are crossed

and that I am in La-La land. I see blackness a lot and have real bad headaches once in a while. Sometimes, but not recently, I get sick and lie in bed thinking, "WHY ME???" Still, it could be worse.

I was diagnosed with occipital seizures in 1991, when I was 7 years old. I went through a lot of EEGs and about three MRIs, which was not a fun thing to do at my age. My eyes dart back and forth, I can't see, and I get scared. At first, I was afraid that one day I might never see the light again. But after having great doctors and medicine (that I don't like to take!), I live with it and just pray that one day they will stop just like they started.

My feelings about my seizures from Day One are very strong. They have affected me very emotionally. Even with my mom and other family members or friends, I get real tense and nervous. Sometimes, like when something really sad happens or has happened, I get real depressed and just feel like crying, or feel like I am nothing. When I get like this, I never blame it on anyone else, especially my mother—she's been wonderful to me.

I get most embarrassed about my seizures in public, like the time my mother and I were visiting my sister in Washington, DC. We were shopping at a mall and were going up an escalator. I was the last to get off and was about halfway up with a drink in my hand and I loudly told my mother, "I'm having a spell!" I dropped my drink. My mother couldn't do anything, since she of course couldn't walk down the escalator which was going up! She just told me to hold the rail. She just grabbed me as soon as she could. I felt very tired. That ended the shopping spree.

Everyone is always so understanding, except me. My eyes feel like they are crossing and then I just can't see. It doesn't last long but they are very real.

I had a great doctor and he was more than just a doctor. He was a friend to me. I met him at the medical center. He made this videotape so I could see what I looked like while having a seizure. I could see that I could still talk and hear. The day I got videotaped, I had about 10 seizures. The doctor got my medication straightened out. He was always there when my mom called him, so we really trusted him.

(*Mother*) It all started in the summer, about 5 years ago. My daughter Kristin was over at my mother's house. Kristin explained to me that she was looking out the window when all of a sudden everything went black. It lasted only a few seconds. At first I thought that she was just blinded by the glare of the sun, but when it happened a few more times within a couple of weeks, I got worried. She would tell me, "Mama, I'm going blind again." They would last about a minute but seemed like much longer! This was very scary for her, and I was terrified that she had a brain tumor! I took her to a family doctor, who had her get an MRI. This was very scary for a 7-year-old. She had to lie completely still for an hour in a long, noisy tube. The outcome was that there was no tumor, but they couldn't make any diagnosis, except perhaps migraines. She had not had any headaches, so of course I wasn't satisfied.

The blind spells continued, so the doctor set her up for an EEG. This wasn't easy either, with glue and little probes all over her head. The EEG showed nothing, so now we were back to where we stared.

Kristin was having more and more of these episodes and they were getting more serious. She started having them daily. Sometimes she would get sick to her stomach afterwards. Her eyes would always dart back and forth. But she could hear you and would talk during a spell, unless it was a very bad one. She would cry and so would I, but I didn't let her see me cry.

Finally, I had my family doctor make us an appointment at the nearby medical center. They got us in right away and scheduled another EEG for the same day. Kristin's doctor was the most wonderful, understanding human being I have ever met. He was very thorough with Kristin and spoke to Kristin and me in terms we could understand. Remarkably, during the EEG she had a spell! We found out then and there that they were seizures. The doctor showed us very clearly on the EEG where it was happening, and how hyperventilation and the strobe lights brought the seizure on. The doctor explained about the medications that could be used and that it might take a while for the dose to be just right for her.

I don't know how many times we went down to the medical center and how many times I had to call the doctor over the next few weeks and months, but it was many, many times. He always got Kristin in right away and kept in close contact with us. The seizures got worse before they got better, sometimes 10 times a day, but finally they came under control.

Kristin was embarrassed about her seizures at first. She seems to have gotten over that. Now she just wants to get off the medications. She takes two kinds, for a total of eight pills a day. I am afraid to let her ride her bike or swim. She gets some sort of feeling before a seizure happens, but it doesn't come soon enough for her to get off her bike if she has to. She takes ballet, and every year, at her recital, I just pray she won't have a seizure. She has to remember to take her pills when she is away from home, which is a lot of responsibility because not everyone is used to someone who must take pills at certain times every day.

Still, she is a great child. She does well in school and is well liked by her friends (and, recently, especially boys). No one ever makes fun of her and she never makes fun of others. This experience has taught her that everyone is different and that things could be worse. I just thank her doctor for all that he has done. We miss him so much since he moved away. He is such a wonderful neurologist. He was the one who found the reason for Kristin's blind spells.

44

(*Mother*) My 4-year-old son ''maybe'' has seizures and maybe not. The doctor thinks he is developing too normally and that is certainly reassuring, but somehow I have an aching, uneasy feeling that he may not be right. I have witnessed enough of the events in question to worry, regardless of whether he is diagnosed or put on seizure medications. I, too, was a child who developed "too normally" to have seizures. In fact, when I was finally diagnosed with seizures and begun on medicine at age 7, I still wasn't told that I had epilepsy—just a "possible seizure disorder."

I am a parent who has epilepsy and I am also a nurse, so the doctors feel that I overreact. Maybe I do, but I have a right to—he is my son! I often feel caught in a dilemma. If I *don't* observe his behavior, or follow up with his day-care teacher about what to report, I ignore a potential problem and place his future in jeopardy. If I *do* report my observations, and make sure others know what to look for and do, they feel that I may be worrying too much or overreacting. What am I, as a parent, supposed to do?

My son had some events with staring and arm shaking when he was 3 or 4 months old, but I ignored them. Couldn't be anything, I thought. But when he was 6 months old his daycare teacher reported episodes of stiffening and shaking of his arms. This was enough for me to have him seen by a neurologist. Everything looked good, and I was told it probably wasn't a seizure and not to worry. Relief! Or was it? He had some funny events over the next few months, nothing to think twice about except in retrospect. One day when he was 8 months old my husband picked him up from daycare so I could catch up on work. When I came home, there was a note from his daycare teacher describing an event in which he was found gasping for breath, with a grayish-blue color, nonresponsive, and then was confused. And no one called me??!! I was scared, furious, and overwhelmed! It just couldn't be happening to him! I frantically called the neurologist, who kindly listened and set up a series of tests over the next few days.

Going through those tests, restraining an 8-month-old, and trying not to panic was not easy. Being a professional in the field made it worse in many ways. I feared that I would not be believed because I knew too much. I was actually quite relieved that the event had happened at daycare—at least someone else had observed it. Again, we were lucky. The tests were normal, and we decided that medicines were not indicated at this time. But that aching, uneasy fear remained.

Over the past 2 years my son has done quite well. He has grown into a beautiful little boy. He has had some unusual events that I suspect are seizures. He has had brief staring episodes, alone or with arm shaking or eye blinking, and even some in which his eyes, arms, or whole body turn to one side. These have been witnessed at home, by my sister, and at daycare. But they are so infrequent. He may go for months without anything, then have a few events over a number of days or weeks. I have noticed a pattern, however, in that they tend to occur when he is coming down with an ear infection. And he has had plenty of those in his short life!

This year, everything was going well until the ear infections began acting up again after the "tubes" fell out. A few months ago, the director of his daycare reported a suspected seizure to me and I witnessed a few very unusual staring events. Then his teacher reported that he tends to be inattentive and "vague" at times. Well, all children can be that way, but as a parent of a child with possible seizures I certainly didn't want to hear that! Is he having more events than we are aware of? Will he have learning troubles? What is going on? Is this all related to his hearing and frequent ear infections? This list of questions is endless.

So I called the neurologist again. This time, I asked him if he thought that I was overreacting and he said "yes." I needed that honest response. I sat back and looked at the whole situation. Why bother putting my son through another EEG right now? What would it change? Regardless of the diagnosis, I agree with the doctor in that I don't want to treat him right now. He is developing well in all other respects, and even the concerns of his daycare teacher about his attention and learning abilities have resolved, at least for now.

But how can I not worry? What about that aching, uneasy feeling? If he is going to have epilepsy we will find out soon enough, and we will deal with it, just as we have coped with my own epilepsy. I don't want him to go through what I have had to, but it is not up to me. Someone up there is making the decisions and I just need to remember that things happen for a reason, and that we will cope with whatever comes our way. It is okay to not like it, as seizures (or whatever) aren't fun and can be scary.

Epilepsy doesn't have to rule our lives—as long as we have people who will listen to us, believe us, and give us honest answers.

45

(Age 20)   It all started one summer about 13 years ago when I was diagnosed with epilepsy. The first medication I took worked well for me until I grew out of it 9 years later. At that point in my life I wanted to be a normal teenager, and that meant ignoring my seizures. I struggled with keeping my seizures from interfering with my last 2 years of high school. I put off having much-needed medical attention and somehow managed to keep going.

During those years I felt out of control, and could not handle my courses at college and having a part-time job at the same time. I kept everything to myself and would not ask for help from my parents. I did not want to deal with the medical disorder.

Finally, I knew there was no running away from myself any longer. My family immediately supported me and I was able to get excellent medical care. It was worth it! Today I am completely seizure-free.

I've been influenced in many positive ways by what has happened to me. I have learned to take responsibility for myself, to get in touch with my feelings, and to look more clearly into the future. I've recently become interested in special education and the possibility of working in the health care field. I hope to be able to help others. I will be returning to college in the fall.

(Mother)   My daughter's first seizure occurred when she was 8 years old. It was the summer. I was several rooms away when I heard strange noises coming from her bedroom. The sound of her teeth banging together stands out in my mind. The seizure lasted 2 to 3 minutes. I felt total fear and helplessness. That afternoon she was diagnosed with a minor seizure disorder and she was started on medication.

The seizures, so it seemed, were completely controlled with medication. We were told she would probably grow out of it all together. She grew into a beautiful, active teenager and was on the swim team and the honor roll. In her sophomore year she began to have staring seizures. We first thought she was daydreaming. The medication was adjusted. She was having other types of seizures which we mistook for difficult behavior. She became forgetful, unfocused, irresponsible, and rebellious. She kept her seizures and inner struggle to herself so as to appear to be a normal teenager. In reality, our family was in turmoil.

She managed to attend college, but her behavior was a problem and we thought she had become involved with drugs. We tried everything and she withdrew further from us.

When her life became completely out of control, she returned to us. She was angry, irrational, and extremely overweight. At that point none of the drugs was working, she was having a wide variety of seizures daily, and her behavior was bizarre. Watching my daughter have these seizures was very painful for me. To see her totally unreachable and in her own world broke my heart. Right after seizures she would become very difficult and verbally abusive. It took me time to learn to stay calm and detached from the verbal abuse. She regressed to being a totally dependent child as we searched for the medical help she needed. There were times when I wondered if that help existed. Then she handed us a book and said we should read it. The book was *Brainstorms: Epilepsy in Our Words*. Looking back, I'm sure it saved our lives.

We are thankful to have found a most wonderful doctor and a new drug that has had profound effects on our daughter's seizures. She is seizure-free, has her life back, and will be returning to college in the fall!

46

(Age 12)   My seizures start with a smell, like vomit. My vision then gets totally black for a few seconds. Then I see a picture in a faraway place. The picture is very bright, but I can't make out what it is. Then the picture gets bigger and bigger and spins towards me (first fast then slow), but just before I'm about to see what it is, it goes away (the seizure stops).

I've had seizures for about 2 years. I'm afraid when it happens. I think I'll be embarrassed if it happens at school. I go to my mom when it happens. I feel better if my mom is around.

(Mother)   When Joe has a seizure, I hold him and try to comfort him. It doesn't affect our lives in that we can't do certain things because of them—we just try to live a normal life. His seizures aren't obvious to other people, and it's hard to explain to friends and relatives because they don't understand. Joe's seizures are not the type where he falls to the ground and shakes. They're more subtle.

My biggest concern now, and always has been, is how do the seizures affect Joe's brain? Does every seizure do some harm to his brain? Does he act the way he does (temper outbursts) because of them? Will it every change? There are a lot of unanswered questions regarding the seizures he gets. I just need to know more. Joe's doctor does his best to explain things, but it seems that there's a lot that doctors don't understand about seizures and the brain.

(Father) I'm not sure how I feel about Joe's seizures. At first I doubted that he was having them. He never comes to me for comfort, so I thought he was doing it for his mother's attention. When I realized what was really happening, I still didn't make too much of it because lots of people have seizures. But I wish that I realized they were seizures sooner so that we could have had them treated sooner.

It's Joe's behavior that really bothers me more, like his rage attacks. Are the seizures playing into these? I just want Joe to get better and have a normal life. I think that if he had a better attitude about things, he could cope with them a little easier.

47

(Mother) Two weeks after my 57-year-old father died suddenly of a massive heart attack while playing volleyball, my 2-year-old son, Tyler, had an unexplained seizure. I was shopping at a department store and Tyler was in a shopping cart. He had been acting somewhat stressed since my father's death, as we all were. Tyler was very close to his grandfather and was trying to accept and understand what his death really meant. I looked away to reach for something on a shelf, and when I turned back to check on him, I noticed that he was staring up towards the ceiling, which wasn't all that unusual. He has always liked to look at the lights on a ceiling. When I looked closer, I noticed that his body was rigid, his back was arched, and his eyes had rolled back. I screamed for help as I took him out of the shopping cart, and two women appeared. Miraculously, both were nurses. One took care of Tyler, laying him on his side on the floor and supporting him as he went into a full convulsion. The other nurse was comforting me, explaining what was happening. She also explained that when the

seizure was over he would probably go into a deep sleep. I was so grateful for this information, because I am sure I would have thought the worst. I was already scared half to death watching my child quivering on the floor.

An ambulance was called. The nurses explained the necessary information to the EMTs when they arrived and Tyler was immediately transported to our local hospital. Both women who had been helping us seemed to disappear after the EMTs arrived, and I was never able to thank them. It left me with the feeling that they were guardian angels, sent down to watch over us. It was a very spiritual feeling.

Tyler's first seizure was last fall. A CT scan and EEG were performed, along with a series of blood tests. All of the test results were inconclusive. It wasn't until my husband met me at the hospital that I remembered him telling me that he had a history of seizures when he was a young child. My husband's first seizure occurred when he was 2 years old and was immediately treated with medication. He remained on the medication until he was 6, even though he only had a few seizures in the first year. He outgrew it. With this information, we were optimistic about Tyler's condition.

Three weeks later Tyler had another seizure, and was hospitalized for more tests and observation, but there were still no conclusive results. He was put on medication. Then the seizures became more frequent, about every 2 weeks. He went on different medications. We made an appointment with a pediatric neurologist. With all the tests coming back inconclusive, the neurologist was in agreement with the treatment Tyler was currently receiving, and is now working with our local neurologist as needed. We were still given optimistic reports about Tyler's condition.

This spring, we finally found the right medication and the right dosage, and Tyler has now been seizure-free for almost 5 months. He is having no harmful side effects from the medication and is doing great.

We know not to be too excited about him growing out of the condition because there are no guarantees, but we are very hopeful.

48

❖ ❖ ❖ ❖ ❖

(Age 12) What does it mean for a kid to have epilepsy? For me, it was a surprise. It means that I have to have blood tests, MRIs, EEGs, CT scans, and go to doctors a lot! The person who takes my blood is now my friend—his name is Bruce. These are things that other kids and some adults don't have to do. Some of them have to do other things, though. Sometimes I am mad that I have to do these things and that I have to take medicine. But the medicine is pretty good at stopping my seizures and that is good.

It feels weird to have a seizure. Sometimes I feel like I'm going to throw up and like something bad is going to happen. Sometimes I smell something coming. It smells really bad, usually. Then I have something that I call a "rememberation." If it is a good memory, it turns bad. If it is a bad memory, it gets worse. A weird thing is I can't remember what the memory was when the rememberation is done. I usually don't feel too good, my stomach hurts or I feel sick, and I am really tired. Then I sleep.

If I have a shiver, sometimes I don't feel anything before and I am surprised by it. Sometimes, I have a really quick hurt stomach or I feel like I am going to throw up. This is real fast. Then I shiver and it is all over. I am not tired.

Other than that, I am a normal girl! I like to dance (actually, I *love* to dance), play basketball, play catch with my brothers and sisters, ride bikes, swim (I love to swim), and collect American Girl stuff. I am learning to bowl. I volunteer two afternoons a week and I will be glad when I can babysit. I love to do puzzles and figure out the times tables my own way. Spinback is my favorite puzzle. I do lots of things.

Sometimes I have to tell other kids why I have to take medicine and what a seizure is. They think that it is scary. I tell them that a seizure is just the brain overfiring. I think that people should know about this. There are even adults who don't!

I like it when people know that I am a girl who has epilepsy, not an *epileptic*. Someday I will be a ballerina and maybe teach children who have epilepsy to dance.

This is such a small part of my life . . . please treat me normally.

Because I am.

(*Mother*) Until 4 years ago, our family life was as normal as that of any family with eight children.

Kathryne, our seventh child, was 7 years old when, out of the blue, she went into status epilepticus and convulsions that lasted about $4\frac{1}{2}$ hours. It was resistant to medications, and she ended up in an intensive care unit on life support for 4 days, followed by another 3 days in a regular pediatrics unit. Very slowly, she came out of the coma. Her memory seemed good, but her motor skills are still recovering 4 years later.

Kate has been suddenly thrust into the world of doctors, medicines, tests, and hospitals. She has very little control of her life, so we try extra hard to let go . . . not easy. The medicine is her responsibility, along with normal things in her life.

She came back to us with a sense of determination that we did not see before this incident. She tries very hard to do everything while still under the influence of various seizure drugs. Two afternoons a week, she volunteers as an aide at a preschool and parenting program. She looks forward to the time when she can babysit. She goes with us when we collect for different charities.

She works hard at balance and coordination, and at minor motor skills. These seem to have been affected by the initial incident. She continues to take dance, as she has since she was 3 years old. She rollerblades, swims, rides bikes . . . all the normal things . . . she has not quite "arrived' yet but continues to play at them and is getting better all the time. She loves basketball and all sorts of group games. We just started bowling as a family thing. She had the chance to be in a TV public service commercial for epilepsy awareness. It is important to Kate for people to know that those who have epilepsy are just as much a part of society as anyone else.

Kate has been through a lot and we are quite proud of her. She came back from the status epilepticus with a different temperament and is nicely surviving a large family and all its oddities. She does not have the social skills that she had before and she is working hard to get them back. She is also trying to get some control on her life.

She is working on a booklet to advise other kids about blood draws! She says, ". . . the most important thing is to know your phlebotomist. Ask him or her how many of these they have done on kids . . . it is good if they have a done a lot of them." She also thinks that it is a good idea to explain in her booklet what they do with the blood in the laboratory to test it. This is interesting to her. She feels that it will help kids to understand why blood draws are important.

Kate's original seizure really frightened her father and me. The chance of it happening again was placed before us as a possibility. This has not happened. Now that she is on a stable medication, she has had a few "rememberations" and "shivers."

Life is not a bed of roses for us, but whose life is? Everyone has challenges; it's just that some are more obvious than others. We feel that Kate certainly has taken that which has been given to her and runs with it! She has been a source of inspiration to many people who were not familiar with epilepsy until they met Kate.

(Father) I think the best way to tell you about my daughter is to start at the beginning with the first seizure that she had when she was 7 years old.

It started with me more like hearing a seizure then seeing it. My wife and two of our daughters had returned from visiting a friend. It was late and I was already in bed. As they talked about the day's activities, our "Winning Kid" fell asleep in her mother's arm and was laying on our living room sofa while my wife was getting our daughter's things ready for bed.

Our older daughter noticed that Katey had spit up. When they tried to arouse her, her response to questions became slower and slower. At this point, they thought that she was teasing them. By this time, I was becoming concerned. I got up and picked her up in my arms, tickling her back to see if she was teasing. After verifying that she was not teasing, I told my wife that we needed to take her to the hospital; luckily for us all, it was only two blocks away.

At the hospital we were questioned as to what was wrong. We could only say that she had spit up and was not responsive to our voices or to tickling her. We were taken to a standard treatment room. In the treatment room, we noticed that one of Katey's pupils was larger than the other and her extremities were starting to contract. We were rushed to a trauma room. The doctor would direct the ER staff and then seem to disappear. Later we found out that he was calling the pediatric trauma center of an affiliated hospital seeking guidance in treatment. Because she had no prior history of seizures or ready explanation for this one, they wanted x-rays to see if there was any head injury or tumor. While the x-rays were being taken, the doctor told us that our daughter might not survive. We went to a chapel where her other siblings, several aunts, grandmother, and family friends were waiting for news. We informed them of what the doctor had said. We all had a feeling of disbelief. There was a lot of trouble comprehending what and why this was happening to Katey.

After the x-rays were read, we were informed that nothing seemed abnormal. We went back to the trauma room, where we continued to see our daughter being breathed artificially, go into a convulsion, and then stop convulsing after medication was given. Then it would start right up again. At one point the staff said for us to call her back because they thought they were losing her. Both my wife, Mary, and I called to her. I turned away, unable to watch. Painted on the wall of the trauma room was the statement "Expect a Miracle." Looking back at the table and seeing the team still working to save my daughter, I prayed that if this child belonged to God, then God's will would be done no matter what the outcome. Just then, Katey stopped seizing.

The ER doctor had called for the affiliated hospital pediatric trauma team to come pick Katey up. They arrived by ambulance and took over all functions being performed on our daughter by the ER staff. As quickly as they came, they loaded our daughter into the ambulance and rolled out the door. Because of the team's size, there was no room for any family member to ride with her to the hospital, which was 45 minutes away. We packed the whole family in the available cars and drove to the affiliated hospital.

We arrived to find that our daughter was alive and not seizing but that she was in a coma in an intensive care pediatric unit. The doctor said that all the tests showed our daughter to be in good health. He warned us that, because of the extended length of the seizure, he could not predict what her condition would be when she came out of the coma. She had been put into a coma on purpose with drugs to stop her seizures.

I was greatly relieved to find that she was alive and in stable condition. I was also concerned about what the future would bring. Since they could not find anything wrong with her, I was optimistic. Mary and I stayed with Katey in the hospital, spelling each other during the night and supporting each other during the days. Katey came back to us with the words "Mom, I need a hug!" She also came back to us with new challenges.

This is what I remember about witnessing my child's first seizure. It has been very hard to write about it. By reliving the events, all the feelings also come back, including the good feeling that you have handled and risen above the crisis to support other members of the family.

Since her first seizure, my daughter has had breakthrough seizures. She has had body tremors and another type of seizure she calls "rememberations," during which she smells "a rotten blueberry aroma," and then she covers her ears, closes her eyes tightly, and curls up into a ball. There is no shaking with this type of seizure. She cannot be aroused, and when she awakens she is extremely tired. We let her rest and make an entry in the journal that we use to keep track of her seizure activity.

My feeling during all of these seizures is one of deep concern. I am also ready to act, if action is required. At first, because of the severity of our daughter's initial seizure, we actually stood watch over her 24 hours a day. Now, with experience, knowledge of the disorder, different medication, and witnessing seizures that stopped without any additional medical involvement, we no longer keep the watch.

We have seen three different neurologists and now are satisfied with the care our daughter is getting. She is on her third medication, which for the most part is controlling her seizure activity. Because of the side affects of her medication, we have tried to lower the dosage.

We have learned that a seizure disorder is diagnosed from the observations made by parents or caregivers, which are then reported to the doctor. Few seizures are observed by the attending physician.

As parents, we are trying to give our daughter as normal a life as possible, allowing her to achieve her dreams and be the best that she can be. With the help of our local epilepsy association, the EFA, and fellow parents, we feel that we are accomplishing these goals. To do this, we are taking life one day at a time.

Thank you for this opportunity to share our story with you.

49

(Mother) I had just put the baby down and went in to kiss my boys. They had gone to bed about 10 minutes before. I turned on their light and was relieved to see that at least one of them was still awake. He was lying on his side with one eye half open and his mouth pulled up on one side, in sort of a grimace. Oh, boys will be boys! He and his brother were always making gross faces and weird noises.

I had to watch where I was walking because so many of their toys were on the floor. When I reached the top bunk he was still playing, or so I thought. "That's really a gross face

. . . cut it out," I said. I went on talking to him and then asked him a question. He didn't answer me. "It's not funny, cut it out," and I grabbed him by the shoulder. His body was stiff and twitching so slightly that I had not even noticed until I touched him.

I screamed for my husband. He came running, alarmed at my voice. I told him our son was having a seizure or something. My husband was very impatient and said, "No, he's not." I then yelled hysterically. "Yes he is. Pick him up and you will see." My husband pulled our son out of bed and found he couldn't hold him over his shoulder or cradle him in both arms because he was so stiff. He had to hold him diagonally. He told me to stop crying and to pray. I tried, but as I saw my son becoming conscious, I walked out of the room so he wouldn't see me upset.

Our pediatrician wanted to put our son on an anticonvulsant immediately. I had just read an article about a particular drug that could cause potentially fatal anemia. I refused to allow my son to take any medication, since he had only had one seizure. After all, I reasoned, he had been in a hot tub the night before the seizure. Perhaps he had gotten overheated.

After that, however, our son seemed rebellious. He didn't do things he was asked to do, claiming that he didn't remember, so he was disciplined. Eight months after the seizure I had witnessed, the school called us. Our son was wandering out of class and didn't know where he was going. I knew immediately he must be having small seizures that we couldn't see, and we were referred to a pediatric neurologist at my request. Nine months after his first seizure he was diagnosed with a "seizure disorder."

I felt guilty because I had refused to allow him to be prescribed the seizure medicine. And I unknowingly punished him for being unconscious! Although I had just weaned the baby in order to go back to work, I decided I didn't want a nanny taking my son for the CT scans, x-rays, blood work, MRIs, and EEGs that he had to have. So I put off going back to work.

For the next 2 years my son was pumped full of all sorts of

medications in the quest to find one that would stop the seizures. Every 2 weeks his little arm was poked to draw blood. At first, none of the medicines seemed to stop his seizures. One time he was standing, laughing uncontrollably with a friend. I could see that he'd wet his pants. I picked him up and carried him into the bathroom. He had defecated as well. I didn't know what was happening. I had the baby and a 6-year-old to take care of as well and I felt overwhelmed. I started yelling as I pulled off his clothes. The poor kid had a seizure and I made him feel ashamed for something he couldn't control.

He had never been allergic to anything. All of a sudden, he was allergic to every medicine we tried. In the middle of all this, we discovered he was now also allergic to sulfa! Every allergic reaction was severe, so the medication would be stopped instantly, and that often caused him to have another seizure. New drugs went into him to offset each allergic reaction, with trips back and forth to doctors dragging the other two kids with me. I had to keep him out of school because he had rashes even in his eyes and mouth. Eventually we found one that controlled the seizures. Unfortunately the side effects were only slightly better than the seizures. One of them was attention deficit disorder (ADD).

I struggled—alone and completely ignorant. Then, during a consultation with a psychiatrist, the word "epilepsy" was used in reference to our son. I said, "No. He doesn't have *epilepsy*. He has a *seizure disorder*."

But I stood corrected. Almost 3 years after that first seizure, I learned that it was epilepsy. Our doctor hadn't told us because of the stigma associated with the word. But how do you find out about "seizure disorder?" It's not listed in the yellow pages. I ran home and found the number of the Epilepsy Association in Los Angeles. They were the first group that sent me written information about epilepsy.

When the doctor recommended we have our child see a psychologist, the only reason she gave was that children with epilepsy often have behavioral problems. She should have insisted we all see one on a regular basis.

Our oldest son could no longer function as the oldest. The medicine sedated him. What a normal child could do in 3 minutes now took him 8. Appointments with specialists took up more of his time. The ADD made it impossible for him to remember much of anything until after the ADD medicine had taken effect. He could no longer meet the responsibilities of the eldest as he had before. He was struggling with the seizures and the effects of the medications on his body and personality. He not only had lost the 2-year lead that he had on his grade level, but he was now falling behind in school. I tried to encourage him by saying that if he worked hard he'd be rewarded for his efforts. He went to the school nurse weekly with stomach pains and nausea and headaches. She'd let him lie down and he'd sleep the rest of the day. I told the school to stop letting him lie down, give him Tylenol for the headache, and send him back to class. These were side effects of the medications and were not going to go away, so I felt that he had to learn to function with them. Still, it broke my heart, because the school thought I was being unreasonable.

The side effects affected him in many other ways. He loved the piano—now he couldn't remember the notes. He was great in sports—now he couldn't concentrate on the game, then he tired too easily, and eventually he was just too small and frail. His mind wouldn't work right and his hands shook. His pupils were always dilated. There were 2 years during which he was so depressed that he wanted to die. He begged me not to send him to school. He said it was like going to hell. I held him while he cried and sent him anyway.

Our middle child became the one everyone relied on to one degree or another. He was 6. During those years when his brother's seizures were not controlled, he had to stop whatever he was doing to follow his brother whenever he went out the front door. He had to help with his baby sister because I was helping his brother and trying to get dinner. One summer, at camp, he joined the other boys in their cabin in ganging up on his brother. If he defended his brother, the boys turned their hostility on him, too, and he couldn't take it. Besides, he said his brother was acting like a jerk. (The counselor did not give the drugs for the ADD.)

Until I went back to work, my daughter got nothing but hand-me-downs because of all the extra costs relating to her brother's needs. She learned to be very independent. I had no time to baby her. My oldest had become the baby. She was disciplined for copying the same behavior that her oldest brother got away with. How do you explain to a preschooler the difference between behavior due to an illness that is treated with medications and behavior that is done on purpose? From her perspective, her brother looked normal, and therefore he wasn't sick. So why didn't we punish him?

My husband didn't want to talk about our son's condition—not with his family, our neighbors, or anyone. He was not interested in hearing from me anything about epilepsy and didn't want any written information. He didn't seem to remember who our child was before the epilepsy and ADD developed. He did not understand what an aura was and how it could turn into a complex partial seizure. He could not distinguish the change in our child's personality and ability due to the medications, and felt that our son should be able to completely control his behavior. He didn't think we should spend any money on therapy.

Everything became so difficult. There were so many problems and somehow, in my husband's mind, our son, and not the epilepsy, was the problem. My husband was very angry with the way our child did or didn't do almost everything. So he passed him over and asked our middle son to help out, because he could accomplish the task better and more quickly.

This dynamic within our family caused our son to "learn" helplessness, shame, anger, withdrawal, and isolation. All of these were devastating to his self-esteem.

Dealing with the school was particularly hard, I could hardly wait to take the pamphlets from the Epilepsy Association to my son's school. I handed them to the teachers and to the principal. I thought that they would be understanding, helpful, and compassionate. I was wrong. They were ignorant and fearful. Even knowing that my son's seizures were still uncontrolled the school officials would not give my son any consideration, saying that to do so would be unfair to the other children. Even though the fifth graders were studying brain cells, the school refused to talk about epilepsy or to mention that my son had it. I knew instinctively that if they would, then my son's classmates would be more supportive and less cruel. But the principal wanted us to put him in a school that my son was "better suited for." After all, he said that my son "is ruining our national test scores and I don't want my students witnessing a grand mal."

I knew that my son had a chance of outgrowing epilepsy, so despite the principal's "advice," I decided to keep my son in normal private schools. That way, he wouldn't think of himself as handicapped. Still, I had my moments of doubt. Was I putting too much pressure on him? Was I unrealistic in my expectations?

Although the educators in the next school were sweet, loving people, they also would not educate the other students about epilepsy or give my son extra time on tests. As a result (I believe), my son was teased, tripped, and hit repeatedly just about every week. He begged me not to interfere. All I could do was talk to the teachers, quietly.

When the time came for him to go to high school, we applied to four schools. As part of the application process, he was time-tested even though I had supplied documentation regarding his two learning disabilities. Three of the schools rejected my son's application. They said that we should put him in a "special" school.

But a neuropsychologist did not agree. She felt he should be mainstreamed because of his above-average intelligence and his incredible tenacity and desire to do well. Fortunately, the fourth school accepted my son and agreed to give him extra time on tests if he needed it. By his second year he made the honor roll. Still, his tutor and I had to intervene many times. We had to educate each new teacher—they never read the report that was in his record. But our son wasn't hit once at this school, and he finally made friends his last year. In spite of everything, our son managed to graduate with his class.

By some miracle, I had done the right thing! I only wish he himself could really understand what he accomplished.

50

(Age 15) Having epilepsy has affected my life in many different ways. For example, when I have to take off from school to go to the doctor, my grades are affected because I have to turn my homework assignments in late. Having epilepsy also makes my friends scared of me and this affects my social life. My friends feel afraid because they won't know what to do if I were to have a seizure. It's also hard to explain to people why I have to take medicine. Many people just don't understand and it takes a long time to explain.

My medicine sometimes gives me bad headaches. It makes me sleepy in the afternoon and that makes it hard to stay awake during school.

Having epilepsy takes away many advantages in my life. I won't be able to get my driver's license unless I am seizure-free for 2 years. I also can't go places without my mom or dad with me.

I wish I didn't have epilepsy, but it's just something I will have to live with until it goes away.

51

❖ ❖ ❖ ❖ ❖

(Mother) As I watched my three-year-old son have his first seizure, I felt like my world had fallen apart. Now, 22 years

later, despite three admissions for invasive monitoring, EEGs, MRIs, CT scans, even a lobectomy, my son will still never live a seizure-free life. We have been through all the medications, we have kept all the blood levels perfect, and we have been through all of the unusual side effects. The best of doctors, medications, and diagnostic tests cannot take away the nightmare that my son has dealt with nearly his entire life.

Recently, I sat with my son at the hospital waiting for him to have a seizure (the one thing I fear most for my son) because he was having a new test, called a SPECT scan. This type of scan is designed to show if there is a "hot spot"—part of the brain that causes seizures and could be removed. When the test was scheduled, we had some reason to be hopeful.

It seemed like it took forever for him to have a seizure so the test could proceed. While I waited with him, I had no sleep, my stomach was growling, and I had headaches. I watched with one eye opened and the other eye closed as the seconds ticked away.

It finally happened! My son had the seizure! He was rushed to the nuclear medicine department to have the necessary injection for the SPECT scan. My heart began to bleed with anticipation as the technicians wheeled him into the scanning room. But then there was more waiting. Will the "hot spot" be found? If not, will our family have to continue to live like this for the rest of our lives? When will we know something? Will another lobectomy be possible? When will the results be back? Where is the doctor?

After more waiting, the results were in. The doctor looked down at his feet and said, "We did find a hot spot, but there are three of them. I'm sorry, but these results mean that your son will never be free of seizures."

I fell to my knees. The moment that we have been waiting for had just turned into the most regretful words that we ever heard. My mind felt like a tornado. What do we do now? What can we do? The answer was *nothing*.

Now we just live for the moment. We hope for a seizure-free day; we wish that the side effects of the medication will get better; and we pray for a cure. We dream that these innocent and special people will have no seizures. We hope that people will accept them for what they are, who they are, and the condition that they have—epilepsy.

We as parents can only do one thing. We can give our children hopes, dreams, and a future, and we can feed them love and encouragement every second of their lives. In our case, our doctors and nurses are a part of this love and encouragement. These trained professionals do their jobs far and beyond human limits. The entire staff has nourished us with the love and sympathy that we were hungry for.

Now, as parents of a child who has severe seizures, we finally accept that our lives will be different. With love, hope, and prayer for our children, we place our trust in the hands of God, who without a doubt will continue to guide the dedicated professionals, support groups, and scientists searching for new tests and medications. Meanwhile, we will go on each day, quietly waiting for the dream to become reality—the dream that these special people will be seizure-free.

To all the parents and family members who live with these seizures, remember—there are many of us who feel alone, sad, and sometimes even frightened. You are *not* alone. Reach out to others in the same position and accept their good will and powerful love. Learn to care, to give of yourselves, and to spread knowledge. And thank God for each new day.

Live for *today*—maybe it will be seizure-free—for tomorrow may never come.

52

❖ ❖ ❖ ❖ ❖

(*Age 17*)   I'm 17 now. I was raised on a beautiful farm. My family is beautiful, too. Sure, we have our troubles, but we are closer to each other than other people I know, by far.

Growing up, I had the best of friends, and the best of girlfriends, too. For a long time, it seemed like my life was perfect. For example, in sports, I was always one of the best athletes, no matter what the sport was (except soccer). I was always able to quickly make friends because I was good in sports. Thank the Lord for my athletic talent because it earned me my friends' respect. It's in the nature of some people when they compete, I believe, to always test their skills and their heart and to give more than 100%. I'm one of those people. I always gave my best, all the time.

But when I developed seizures a couple of years ago, it seemed like I lost everything. At first, my life was shattered, because I felt like I was starting all over again from scratch. It was like being a 5-year-old in a 15-year-old's body. Soon after I was diagnosed with epilepsy, I was put on what seemed like a hundred medications. All of them made me feel like crap. I lost a lot of faith because of this. I asked myself many questions, but most of all, I wondered ''What did I do to deserve this?'' I was also upset about the fact that the seizures took away my chance to play college football, and I loved football dearly. I felt like I couldn't go out to places without worrying that something would go wrong with me. I was scared that my friends would think that I was messed up. I quickly found out who my real friends were.

My girlfriend at that time helped me more than anyone else. Her care for me made me realize how important it was to have someone by your side who loves you. I still wonder if she stayed with me out of love or because of pity.

Since then, things have gotten better. I found out that you must stand up and take control of your life. Don't worry about every minor detail. Be happy with those things that you have rather than the things you can't or don't have.

In my case, my prayers were answered—I'm playing football again and my medicines have all been squared away. As for my friends, I don't waste any time on people who aren't true friends. I found that my true friends quickly understood my problems and cared about me as a person; some of them also had problems themselves.

As I look back on everything, I realize that epilepsy was

hard to deal with in the beginning but that over time it got easier to cope with. It has made me a very strong person. My ability to overcome problems is amazing to me, and I credit my epilepsy with teaching me how to do it.

53

(Age 17) One fall day during my ninth grade health class, something happened that changed my life—I had my first convulsion.

No one in class knew what had happened to me. The ambulance took me to the hospital and after many tests, the doctors released me saying that they couldn't find anything wrong with me.

However, the seizures continued on a regular basis, along with other, milder seizures that happened every day. Yet each and every time I went to a doctor, I would be told that everything was normal and I would be sent home. It was truly frustrating. One doctor put me on medicines that I was allergic to.

We didn't know where to turn. Then we were introduced to a doctor at the university epilepsy center. He was the first doctor who I felt took me seriously. He told me that he, too, didn't know what was going on, but that he was willing to find out and to work with me. After I had several more seizures, I was admitted to the epilepsy ward for monitoring. He found that I was having two types of seizures.

The first medicine that he tried didn't work that well and I gained a lot of weight and didn't feel well. But my doctor didn't give up. Together we worked through different medicines. Today I take a combination of medicines that control my seizures. I haven't had a seizure in over 7 months!

I am now ending my junior year in high school. I take my

medicines faithfully and see my doctor for regular check-ups. My doctor was wonderful with me through the difficult years. He was always there for me, supporting me like a friend I could count on. He was always honest with me and I trusted him.

Presently, I feel energetic and seizures are the least of my worries. I enjoy doing sports and just having fun with my family and friends. Yes, I'm still careful about things because of the possibility that I might have a seizure, but hey, I have to live up to my current title, which is "Teenager!" So, if you want to describe me, well I'm no different than any other teenager—thanks to my doctor.

54

(Mother)   My daughter was diagnosed with epilepsy 2 years ago when she was 15. I awoke when Jeremy said, "Mom, come here, I think there is a burglar and Corey is hurt. Something is wrong, Mom. Hurry!" Well, it turned out that Jeremy heard a guttural sound, a thud, and some banging, and assumed that we had a thief in our presence. I wish to this day that had turned out to be the case instead of Corey having a seizure.

Corey was soon diagnosed with epilepsy and has been on medication since then. She has responded well since the correct dosage was found.

Corey is employed at a pharmacy. Her pharmacist sent her home with *Brainstorms: Epilepsy in Our Words,* a book about people and their seizures. This is the only material I have ever read on the subject of seizures that is written with such compassion and honesty. I feel privileged to have read it and relieved to see that the many emotions I still experience are common to other families. I was especially interested in the writings of other mothers, as I find the feeling of guilt to be overwhelming. I pray that God will take this from her and give it to me.

We all seem to find humor in any situation we are confronted with, and at times this is just how we deal with the seizures. Occasionally we call my daughter "Flounder." Of course we are teasing her, but we say it with love. We don't want this to be a horrible thing that has happened to her. We want her to understand that this is simply a part of her life and a part of our life also. She is not different, she just has to take extra care of herself, as we all should.

She has just recently been granted a driver's license, and this is a point of anxiety for me. I think that I have taught her to be responsible and hope that if she is feeling "funny" on any given day she will not drive, but the fear of an accident has become a constant concern for me. After all, she is only 17 and we are all immortal when we are 17, or so we think. I want her to experience the same things other teens experience. I want her to feel the same and understand that she is the same—she just has a seizure disorder.

The hard part is dealing with the fears of the "uneducated," the stigma of mental illness, the stigma of being weird, and the stigma of impairment that those people apply to persons with epilepsy. Well, none of that applies to *my* daughter. She is a beautiful, intelligent young woman with as much of a chance for a wonderful future as anyone else.

I have always believed in my child. I hope that this book will reinforce the same belief in you about your child.

Guide for Teachers and Parents

William Murphy

❖ ❖ ❖ ❖ ❖

For most students, school offers a safe, accepting, and nurturing environment. For a student with epilepsy, his or her sense of safety, acceptance, and opportunity is influenced by others' understanding of the disorder, their response to seizures, and their expectations of the student. The unpredictable nature of epilepsy means that teachers—indeed, all school personnel—and other students may suddenly, without warning, have to respond to a seizure at school. The student who has a seizure at school may face a range of consequences and reactions to the episode, including embarrassment, fear, rejection, and interference with the learning process. Including epilepsy education and awareness in the school curriculum can minimize these consequences and help to assure everyone that epilepsy and seizures can be dealt with appropriately.

The School Alert program of the Epilepsy Foundation of America (EFA) and its network of national affiliates offers a variety of materials and strategies for educating school personnel and students about epilepsy. Inviting a person who is knowledgeable about epilepsy to be a speaker at the school can increase everyone's confidence in their ability to respond to a seizure and their understanding of the concerns a person with epilepsy may have. In turn, these benefits will help the student with epilepsy to feel more secure and accepted, and will reduce parents' concerns for their child's safety and general wellbeing while in school. Excellent materials for use in a school epilepsy program are readily available through EFA (1-800-EFA-1000) and its local affiliates. The flexibility of format and variety of content of these materials make them suitable for any school setting and age level. Reaching thousands of students and school staff each year, epilepsy education programs all have the goal of improving the school environment for the student who has epilepsy. Having an epilepsy expert meet with students and staff offers opportunities for the speaker to provide basic epilepsy education and to address specific concerns the audience may have about dealing effectively with epilepsy in a school setting.

The benefits of a coordinated School Alert program, including outreach, organized content, and a cadre of trained and knowledgeable speakers, are apparent. However, even in the absence of a local epilepsy organization to implement an ongoing School Alert program, parents and schools nationwide can access the materials, including an array of videos and manuals, to learn about epilepsy.

Too often, epilepsy education is provided only *after* a student has a seizure at school. Such common reactions as fear, helplessness, and genuine concern for the student's safety initiate an epilepsy awareness program. Certainly a better approach would be to teach students and staff *beforehand* how to respond to seizures and to those who have them. First, however, the availability of and the need for such a program must be brought to the attention of school faculty and administration. The parents of a child with epilepsy should be encouraged to notify the school of their child's epilepsy and how best to respond if a seizure occurs in school. Consistency in the response to a seizure at school and at home increases the child's sense of security and avoids sending the child mixed messages about what a seizure is and how to deal with it. Parents should also encourage school administrators to contact the local epilepsy organization to request a School Alert program. If administrators express any hesitancy in doing so, parents can offer to contact the epilepsy group to schedule a program. This approach demonstrates the parents' strong desire to have the program and a willingness to work with the school. In the absence of a local epilepsy organization, parents can offer to work with the appropriate school personnel, typically a school nurse or health educator, to gather and review available materials and help plan a presentation. When promoting the program to a school, parents or the local epilepsy organization should point out that epilepsy is one of the most common chronic neurological disorders and one with which all school personnel should be familiar. It is estimated that between one and two percent of the population has epilepsy. Given that more than 60 percent of persons with epilepsy develop seizures before young adulthood, the chances are that every teacher has had or will have a child with epilepsy in his or her class. In addition, epilepsy education programs encourage tolerance of individual differences and provide a basic health/science lesson on how the brain and the central nervous system work. The possibility that an epilepsy education program may be approved for continuing education credit for teachers, school nurses, social workers, and other professionals in a school may also induce school officials to implement the program.

A School Alert program provides a general overview of epilepsy and approaches to dealing with common concerns about the disorder. It is not intended, nor should it be, to draw attention to any particular student or to provide medical advice or answers to specific individual needs. If a program is offered in a classroom or school in which a child is known to have a seizure disorder, it is recommended that the student and the child's parents be informed of the program and asked for their input to ensure that the program has a positive impact on the child. Very often, parents and students with epilepsy are willing to participate in epilepsy education programs to describe first-hand their experiences in living with epilepsy and how they prefer a seizure to be handled. Program content will depend on the audience, of course, and audiences will vary. The ideal is to offer a classroom presentation for students and a separate in-service program for school personnel.

An excellent resource for educating students about epilepsy is the manual *Teaching Students About Epilepsy* developed by the Program Actions for Children with Epilepsy (PACE) program at the Good Samaritan Hospital and Medical Center of Portland, Oregon. This manual offers an epilepsy education curriculum and student worksheets for different grade levels. The lessons can be supplemented with age-appropriate videos that aid in telling students what epilepsy is, how best to help someone having a seizure, and the importance of being that person's friend. Classroom presentations are enhanced by including a person who has epilepsy as a guest speaker. Students can then ask questions and get answers based on the speaker's first-hand experience. Many schools and epilepsy organizations extend the program to include a "Kids on the Block" puppet show or an essay/poster contest. Creative components add fun and incentives to the program, and the opportunities are limitless.

The content of in-service programs for school personnel should have greater depth. In addition to providing basic information on epilepsy and first aid, an effective program should offer strategies for dealing with epilepsy in a school setting. It should address the impact epilepsy may have on the educational, social, and vocational development of a student and should include suggestions for assessment and appropriate interventions. Speakers need to be knowledgeable about the topics, well prepared, and comfortable with public speaking. Ideal candidates to recruit as speakers include local neurologists, epilepsy nurse specialists and other neuroscience nurses, social workers, staff members of local epilepsy organizations, and persons who both have epilepsy and are well versed in educational issues.

Suggested topics for a staff presentation follow. Each topic includes opportunities for increasing the school's positive response to epilepsy.

An Overview of Epilepsy and Its Causes:

This includes basic facts about seizures, definitions, and incidence and prevalence of epilepsy. This topic also includes safety and information about daily living habits that may prevent epilepsy.

An Explanation of the Different Types of Seizures:

This includes classification of seizure types, extent and location of brain involvement, observable manifestations of different seizure types, and common seizure triggers. Discussing different seizure types and their outward signs increases a staff's ability to recognize possible seizure activity. The role and importance of teachers' observations should be emphasized because teachers may aid in the early detection of seizures and in recognition of possible seizure triggers. Discussing ways for teachers to share their observations with parents and medical professionals can help in early diagnosis and determination of treatment. In addition, the topic of recognizing seizure triggers can be discussed with students, with the intent of possibly preventing a seizure occurrence.

Appropriate First Aid for Seizures:

This emphasizes that seizures can be dealt with efficiently and in a matter-of-fact way that reassures others of the person's safety. It includes information about secondary injuries and status epilepticus, and helps to establish guidelines for obtaining emergency medical aid.

Treatment Options That Help to Control or Reduce Seizures:

This includes a discussion of treatment compliance and opportunities for students, when appropriate, to assume responsibility for taking their medications. Discussing side effects of medications once again underscores the importance of teachers' observations, encouraging them to look at the variety of factors that may influence a child's academic performance, behavior, and sociability. These factors include the seizures themselves, antiepileptic medications, and anxiety a child may feel about possibly having a seizure. Discussing the array of treatment options, including medications, surgery, special diets, and self-help skills, may also prompt a dialogue, encouraging students whose seizures are not well controlled to consider a medical reevaluation and to utilize comprehensive epilepsy services that are now more widely available.

The Spectrum of Psychosocial Factors and Common Problems Often Associated with Living with Epilepsy:

This includes recommendations for rectifying or possibly minimizing psychosocial concerns. Discussing this topic increases the staff's ability to explain epilepsy to others, promotes acceptance of the student who has epilepsy, and encourages that student to function at full potential. School personnel need to feel comfortable about providing opportunities for students with epilepsy to increase their independence (e.g., taking responsibility for their medication), take appropriate risks (e.g., playing sports), to put their epilepsy in its proper context (e.g., understanding what limitations, if any, their epilepsy presents), and to look at options open to them. Success in providing these components to students with epilepsy helps the child, in turn, to set goals, and can provide a basis in later years for making and attaining long-range vocational plans.

A common concern is the child's participation in recreational activities or tasks that could be considered dangerous, such as chemistry lab experiments. As important as it is to minimize risks, it is also important to remove any unnecessary restrictions. It should be emphasized that a diagnosis of epilepsy does not, in itself, preclude participating in an activity. However, assessing the impact of certain factors on a child's participation in a specific activity can help in the decision-making process. These factors include the child's seizure type and seizure frequency, what happens during a seizure, the presence or absence of an "aura," side effects of medications, and the child's overall level of functioning. Restrictions imposed by parents and/or medical care providers must be honored. As changes in these factors occur, new opportunities may become available to the student. Observation and open communication are keys to the process.

Community Resources:

A child's situation may be further complicated by other medical concerns; learning or cognitive difficulties and social, behavioral, or emotional problems. Families often seek help in understanding laws pertaining to education and in obtaining optimal medical care, financial assistance, and appropriate support services. Providing the best education for some students may require a comprehensive approach through a number of disciplines. Schools may request very specialized assistance in assessing a student's situation and in developing an educational plan. Including a list of medical and support services with epilepsy education materials is helpful to parents and school personnel. The EFA, the local epilepsy organization, and the National Information Center for Children and Youth with Disabilities (1-800-695-0285) can assist in compiling a list of services specific to an area.

As the child with epilepsy grows and progresses in school, his or her concerns change. Common concerns as children mature are the possibility of increased seizure activity, treatment compliance, effects of medication changes, and the influence of puberty and body changes on seizure control. Social issues also change with time. Acceptance and self-esteem are continual concerns for most children with epilepsy. Students, parents, and teachers may have to deal with the impact of seizures on driving privileges, dating, sports, recreational activities, and academic stress, to name a few. It helps to know that, as these issues arise, community resources are available to assist in assessing their impact, to provide information that can help in decision making, and to offer referrals to needed services.

A school epilepsy education program serves as the foundation for an ongoing relationship between children with epilepsy, their peers and teachers, and the community, which can assist in addressing a continuum of issues. The program will benefit many people, but especially students with epilepsy.

Glossary

Georgia D. Montouris

❖ ❖ ❖ ❖ ❖

Absence seizure: formerly called "petit mal" seizure. Form of primary generalized seizure consisting of 5 to 15 seconds of unresponsiveness, occurring without any warning or without any aftermath. Appears much like "daydreaming." Unique EEG pattern: 3 per second spike and wave.

Apgar score: evaluation of a newborn infant's physical status, usually determined after 60 seconds of life. Score is sum of points assigned (0–2) for heart rate, respiratory effort, muscle tone, reflex irritability, and skin color. Maximal score is 10.

Apnea monitor: a machine designed to monitor respiration so as to detect absence of breathing (apnea).

Arteriovenous malformation (AVM): malformation of arteries and veins such that blood is shunted from arteries to veins without passing through the capillary system. Often causes cerebral (brain) hemorrhage and seizures.

Atonic seizure: primary generalized seizure characterized by loss of muscle tone, resulting in a fall to the ground ("drop attack").

Atypical absence seizure: a seizure that clinically resembles an absence seizure but has a different EEG pattern.

Aura: a peculiar sensation experienced by a patient just before a seizure.

AVM: see Arteriovenous malformation.

Brain tumor: a mass or growth within the brain that may or may not be cancerous. Can be the cause of a seizure disorder.

Cardiac: pertaining to the heart.

Clinical drug trial: clinical use of a medication not yet marketed but being tested for its safety and effectiveness under guidelines established by the sponsoring pharmaceutical company and by the Food and Drug Administration.

Complex partial seizure: type of seizure, usually lasting 2 to 5 minutes, and consisting of a glassy stare and an altered state of consciousness. Often accompanied by repetitive movements (automatisms) such as lip smacking, licking, swallowing, or picking motions of the hands. An aura often precedes this type of seizure, and confusion with no recall for the event usually follows. This seizure may precede a convulsive (tonic–clonic) seizure.

Computed tomography scan (CT or CAT scan): a form of imaging that uses a computer to mathematically reconstruct the tissue density of the scanned body part.

Convulsion: also called "grand mal" seizure or tonic–clonic seizure. Characterized by loss of consciousness and stiffening of the body, followed by rhythmic jerking of the limbs, trunk, and head. This type of seizure, which usually lasts less than 5 minutes, often results in falling down, tongue biting, and bladder or bowel incontinence. It is often preceded by an aura and followed by irresistible sleep and/or confusion.

CT scan: see Computed tomography scan.

DPT shot: triple vaccination against diphtheria, pertussis (whooping cough), and tetanus.

Drop attack: see Atonic seizure.

Drop seizure: see Atonic seizure.

EEG: see Electroencephalogram.

EFA: see Epilepsy Foundation of America.

Electroencephalogram (EEG): a device that records the electrical activity of the brain by means of electrodes placed on the scalp.

Emergency medical technician (EMT): a person trained in emergency procedures and usually affiliated with an ambulance team.

EMT: see Emergency medical technician.

Encephalitis: an infection or inflammation of the brain.

Epilepsy Foundation of America (EFA): a national organization that supports patients and families affected by epilepsy, epilepsy research and education, and advocacy for persons with epilepsy.

Epileptologist: a medical doctor (usually a neurologist) who specializes in the diagnosis and treatment of epilepsy.

ER: emergency room.

Febrile seizure: a seizure that occurs only in association with high fever. No abnormalities on a routine EEG are associated with this type of seizure.

Focal motor seizure: a seizure characterized by involvement of only one body part or one side of the body.

Genetic workup: an evaluation to determine whether a person has a hereditary disorder.

Grand mal seizure: see Convulsion.

Hemispherectomy: a specialized type of epilepsy surgery in which almost half of the brain is removed.

Infantile spasm: a seizure characterized by a sudden, jack-knife-life forward thrust of the upper body with arms out. Often called ''salaam attack'' because of the patient's bow-like posture. This type of seizure is usually associated with underlying brain damage.

Intractable seizures: seizures that are not controlled by standard medications. Also called ''refractory seizures.''

Invasive monitoring: continuous inpatient video-telemetry monitoring and recording of onset of seizure activity by use of surgically placed electrode strips or grids over the brain's surface or depth electrodes placed in the brain.

Ketogenic diet: a high-fat diet found effective in the treatment of a small percentage of childhood seizures of a specific type.

Lobectomy: removal of a lobe of the brain. In epilepsy surgery, the lobe that contains the seizure focus is removed.

Long-term monitoring (LTM): continuous video-telemetry in-patient monitoring by use of EEG electrodes placed on the scalp (not surgically placed) and simultaneous recording of clinical seizure activity on video camera.

LTM: see Long-term monitoring.

Magnetic resonance imaging (MRI): a form of imaging that uses a magnetic field and radio waves to produce an anatomically detailed image of a body part.

Metabolic workup: analysis of blood chemistry and urine to detect any abnormality that may account for the cause of seizure activity.

Mixed epilepsy: occurrence of several seizure types in the same patient.

MRI: see Magnetic resonance imaging.

Myoclonic seizure: a seizure characterized by a sudden, brief (less than 1 second) jerk of a limb or the head without loss of consciousness. Can occur as sole seizure type or in combination with either absence or tonic–clonic seizures.

Neurologist: a physician who specializes in disorders of the brain, spinal cord, muscles, and peripheral nerves.

Neuropsychologist: a professional trained to administer and interpret tests of intelligence and cognitive abilities.

Nocturnal seizures: seizures that occur only during sleep.

Nonconvulsive status epilepticus: continuous seizures, without cessation over a prolonged period of time, consisting of either absence or partial seizures, with no apparent convulsive activity.

Obstetrician/gynecologist (OB/GYN): a physician who specializes in women's health and pregnancy.

Occipital lobe: the portion of the brain that controls vision.

PET scan: see Positron emission tomography.

Petit mal seizure: see Absence seizure.

Positron emission tomography (PET): a scan of the brain to evaluate its function. After radionuclides (radioactive substances) are administered to the patient, a scanning device detects the presence of brain metabolites, such as glucose (sugar).

Rasmussen's encephalitis: chronic focal inflammatory changes in the brain that lead to intractable seizures. Hemiparesis is common. Usually occurs before the age of 20.

Refractory seizures: see Intractable seizures.

Simple partial seizure: a seizure during which jerking of a limb or the face may occur, or a subjective feeling occurs. There is no change in consciousness or level of alertness, and the patient can respond to others during the event. May be immediately followed by a complex partial seizure or a convulsion (tonic–clonic seizure).

Status epilepticus: continuous seizure activity lasting longer than 10 minutes. When convulsive, neurologic damage or even death can occur if immediate emergency medical treatment is not given.

Stroke: loss of blood flow to a region of the brain due to blockage of a cerebral blood vessel. Neurologic damage depends on which vessel is involved and where blockage occurs.

Tonic seizure: a seizure characterized by stiffening of the body.

Tonic–clonic seizure: see Convulsion.

Urologist: a physician who specializes in diseases of the kidney and bladder.

Appendix I

Epilepsy Foundation of America (EFA)
Affiliate Listings

❖ ❖ ❖ ❖ ❖

Note: Some EFA affiliate addresses and/or telephone numbers may have changed since this list was prepared. For current information, call 1-800-EFA-1000 for the affiliate nearest you. Or check the affiliate locator (Where We Are) on the EFA's Internet Home Page (www.efa.org).

Alabama

Epilepsy Foundation of
  North and Central Alabama
1801 Oxmoor Road, Suite 101
Birmingham, AL 35209
205-870-1146
800-950-6662

Epilepsy Chapter of
  Mobile and Gulf Coast
951 Government Street, Suite 201
Mobile, AL 36604
334-432-0970
800-626-1582

Arizona

Epilepsy Society of Arizona
PO Box 25084
Phoenix, AZ 85002-5084
602-406-3581

California

Epilepsy Foundation of
  Central California
1069 North Fulton Street
Fresno, CA 93728
209-485-6242

Epilepsy Foundation of
  Northern California
1615 Broadway, Suite 411

Oakland, CA 94612-2124
510-893-6272

Epilepsy Society of
  San Diego County
2055 El Cajon Boulevard
San Diego, CA 92104
619-296-0161

Epilepsy Foundation of Los
  Angeles and Orange Counties
3600 Wilshire Blvd., Suite 920
Los Angeles, CA 90010-2613
231-382-7337
800-564-0445

Epilepsy Society of
  Kern County, Inc.
405 South Chester Avenue
Bakersfield, CA 93304
805-832-9228

Colorado

Epilepsy Foundation of
  Colorado, Inc.
234 Columbine Street, Suite 333
Denver, CO 80206
303-377-9774

Connecticut

Epilepsy Foundation of
  Connecticut, Inc.
1800 Silas Deane Highway, #168

143

Rocky Hill, CT 06067
860-721-9226
800-899-3745

Delaware

Epilepsy Foundation of Delaware
New Castle Corporate Commons
61 Corporate Circle
New Castle, DE 19720
302-324-4455

Subunit:
The Employment & County
  Senior Program
213 W. DuPont Highway
Millsboro, DE 19966
302-934-9857

District of Columbia

Epilepsy Foundation for the
  National Capital Area
1331 H Street, NW, Suite 1005
Washington, DC 20005
202-638-5229

Florida

Epilepsy Foundation of
  West Central Florida, Inc.
4023 North Armenia, Suite 100
Tampa, FL 33607
813-870-3414
813-870-1321 (FAX)

Subunit:
Tri-County Office
225 East Lime Street
Lakeland, FL 33801
813-686-5880

Epilepsy Foundation of
  Southwest Florida, Inc.
40 North Osprey Avenue,
Suite A
Sarasota, FL 34236-8545
941-953-5988

Suncoast Epilepsy Association,
  Inc.
5580 Park Blvd, Suite 4
Pinellas Park, FL 34665
813-546-2856

Subunit:
Clearwater County Office
United Way Services Center
2451 Enterprise Road
Clearwater, FL 34641
813-796-2805

The Epilepsy Foundation of
  Northeast Florida, Inc.
6028 Chester Avenue, Room 106
Jacksonville, FL 32217
904-731-3752

Epilepsy Association of the
  Palm Beaches
5730 Corporate Way, Suite 220
West Palm Beach, FL 33407
407-478-6515
800-940-6515

Epilepsy Foundation of
  South Florida, Inc.
Chase Federal Building
7300 N. Kendall Drive, Suite 700
Miami, FL 33156
305-670-4949, ext. 211

Epilepsy Association of
  Broward County, Inc.
Chamber of Commerce Building
512 NE Third Ave., Suite 301
Fort Lauderdale, FL 33301
954-779-1509

Epilepsy Society of
  Northwest Florida
8 North Coyle Street
Pensacola, FL 32501
904-433-1395

Subunit:
Epilepsy Society of NW Florida
PO Box 1205

Ft. Walton Beach, FL 32549
904-862-1458

Epilepsy Association of
 Central Florida
22 West Lake Beauty Drive
Suite 314
Orlando, FL 32806
407-422-1416

Subunit:
EACF Brevard Co. Office
1600 Sarno Road, #119
Melbourne, FL 32935
407-253-4112

Georgia

Georgia Chapter, EA
100 Edgewood Ave. NE, Suite
 #1200
Atlanta, GA 30303
404-527-7155
800-527-7105

Subunit:
Epilepsy Foundation of
 NW Georgia, Inc.
PO Box 4246
Dalton, GA 30721-1246
706-226-1248

Catoosa, Dade, and Walker
 Counties, GA are served by the
 affiliate listed below:
Epilepsy Foundation of
 Greater Chattanooga
744 McCallie Avenue, Suite 421
Chattanooga, TN 37403
423-756-1771

Hawaii

Epilepsy Foundation of
 Hawaii, Inc.
1833 Kalakaua Avenue, Suite 601
Honolulu, HI 96815-1527
808-951-7705
800-332-4464

Subunit:
Epilepsy Foundation of
 Hawaii–Maui Chapter
3540 Keahi Place
Kihei, HI 96753
808-242-6682

Idaho

Epilepsy League of Idaho
310 West Idaho
Boise, ID 83702
208-344-4340
800-237-6676

Subunit:
ELI Eastern Idaho Outreach
 Office
480 Park Ave., Suite 3A
Idaho Falls, ID 83402
208-529-3580

Illinois

Epilepsy Foundation of
 Southern Illinois
1100 D South 42nd Street
Mt. Vernon, IL 62864
618-244-6680

Epilepsy Association of
 Rock Valley
321 West State Street, Suite 208
Rockford, IL 61101
815-964-2689
800-221-2689

Epilepsy Foundation of
 Greater Chicago
20 East Jackson Boulevard, 13th
 Floor
Chicago, IL 60611
312-939-8622
800-273-6027

Epilepsy Association of
 Southwestern Illinois
1200 Caseyville Avenue
Swansea, IL 62220
618-236-2181

Indiana

Clark and Floyd Counties, are
served by the following
affiliate:
Epilepsy Council of
Greater Cincinnati, Inc.
3 Centennial Plaza
895 Central Avenue
Cincinnati, OH 45202
613-721-2905

Iowa

Harrison, Mills, and
Pottawattamie Counties are
served by the following
affiliate:
Epilepsy Association of Nebraska
6910 Pacific Street, Suite 103
Omaha, NE 68106
402-553-6567
800-477-0290

Kansas

Wyandotte County is served by
the following affiliate:
Epilepsy Foundation for the
Heart of America Region
4949 Rockhill Road
Kansas City, MO 64110
816-276-8940
800-972-5163

Kentucky

Adair, Anderson, Bath Dell,
Boone, Bourbon, Boyd, Boyle,
Bracken, Breathitt, Bullit,
Campbell, Carroll, Carter,
Casey, Clark, Clay, Clinton,
Cumberland, Elliott, Estill,
Fayette, Fleming, Floyd,
Franklin, Gallatin, Garrard,
Grant, Greenup, Hardin,
Harlan, Harrison, Hart, Henry,
Jackson, Jefferson, Jessamine,
Johnson, Kenton, Knott,
Knox, Laurel, Lawrence, Lee,
Leslie, Letcher, Lewis,
Lincoln, McCreary, Madison,
Magoffin, Marion, Martin,
Mason, Menifee, Mercer,
Montgomery, Morgan, Nelson,
Nicholas, Oldham, Owne,
Owsley, Pendleton, Perry,
Pike, Powell, Pulaski,
Robertson, Rockcastle, Rowan,
Russell, Scott, Shelby,
Spencer, Taylor, Trimble,
Washing, Wayne, Whitley,
Wolfe, Woodfo
The counties listed above are
served by this affiliate:
Epilepsy Council of
Greater Cincinnati, Inc.
3 Centennial Plaza
895 Central Avenue
Cincinnati, OH 45202
513-721-2905

Subunit:
Eastern & Central Kentucky
Epilepsy Council of
Greater Cincinnati
205 Main Street
Williamstown, KY 41097
606-824-6699

Subunit:
Epilepsy Association of
Greater Louisville, a program
of the Epilepsy Council of
Greater Cincinnati
334 East Broadway
Louisville, KY 40402
502-584-8817

Subunit:
Eastern & Southern Kentucky
Epilepsy Council of
Greater Cincinnati
22 Bluegrass Road
East Bernstadt, KY 40729
606-843-7811

Subunit:
Warren County Ohio: a program
  of the Epilepsy Council of
  Greater Cincinnati
570 N. State Rte. 741
Lebanon, OH 45036
513-925-2550

Louisiana

Epilepsy Council of SE Louisiana
4840 Banks Street
New Orleans, LA 70119
504-486-6326
800-960-0587

Maryland

Epilepsy Association of Maryland
Hampton Plaza
300 E. Joppa Road, Suite 1103
Towson, MD 21286
410-828-7700
800-492-2523

Subunit:
Epilepsy Association of Maryland
Southern Maryland Office
Parole Professional Center
132 Holiday Court, Suite 206
Annapolis, MD 21401
410-266-7941
800-966-7940

Montgomery County and Prince
  George's County, MD are
  served by the following
  affiliate:
Epilepsy Foundation for the
  National Capital Area
1331 H Street NW, Suite 1005
Washington, DC 20005
202-638-5229

Massachusetts

Epilepsy Association of
  Massachusetts
59 Temple Place, Suite 550

Boston, MA 02111
617-542-2292

Michigan

Epilepsy Center of Michigan
26211 Central Park Blvd., Suite
  100
Southfield, MI 48076
810-351-7979
800-377-6226

Subunit:
Epilepsy Center of
  Michigan Satellite Office
Detroit, MI 48202

Minnesota

Epilepsy Foundation of
  Minnesota
777 Raymond Avenue
St. Paul, MN 55114
612-646-8675
800-779-0777

Subunit:
North Central Minnesota Office
703 Pokegama Avenue North
Grand Rapids, MN 55744
218-327-2128

Epilepsy League of
  Lake Superior, Inc.
4944 Matterhorn Drive
Duluth, MN 55811
218-722-4526
800-637-1542

Mississippi

Epilepsy Foundation of
  Mississippi
4795 McWillie Drive, Suite 101
Jackson, MS 39206
601-362-2761
800-898-0291

Subunit:
Epilepsy Foundation of
  Mississippi
917 Goodyear Blvd, Unit "0"
Picayune, MS 39466
601-798-0184

DeSoto County, MS is served by
  the following affiliate:
Epilepsy Foundation of
  W. Tennessee
1750 Madison Ave., Suite B-40
Memphis, TN 38104
901-272-3268

Missouri

Epilepsy Foundation for the
  Heart of America Region
4949 Rockhill Road
Kansas City, MO 64110
816-276-8940
800-972-5163

Epilepsy Foundation of the
  St. Louis Region
7100 Oakland Avenue
St. Louis, MO 63117-1881
314-645-6969
800-264-6970

Subunit:
Epilepsy Association of the
  Ozarks
309 N. Jefferson, Suite 253
Springfield, MO 65806
417-869-6848

Nebraska

Epilepsy Association of Nebraska
6910 Pacific St., Suite 103
Omaha, NE 68106
402-553-6567
800-477-0290

New Jersey

Epilepsy Foundation of
  New Jersey

50 East State Street, Suite 212
Trenton, NJ 08608
609-392-4900
800-336-5843

Subunit:
Central New Jersey Office
Epilepsy Foundation of
  New Jersey
98 James Street, Suite 313
Edison, NJ 08820
908-321-7015

Subunit:
Southern New Jersey Office
Epilepsy Foundation of NJ
Station House Office Bldg
900 Haddon Ave., Suite 110–112
Collingswood, NJ 08108
609-858-5900

New York

Epilepsy Association of
  Greater Rochester, Inc.
Al Sigl Center, Winton Campus
3399 Winton Road South
Rochester, NY 14623
716-334-6400
800-724-7930

The Epilepsy Foundation of
  Long Island, Inc.
550 Stewart Avenue
Garden City, NY 11530
516-794-5500

Subunit:
Epilepsy Foundation of
  Long Island
Suite 200-B, 2nd Floor
2100 Middle Country Road
Centerreach, NY 11720
516-467-3989

Epilepsy Society of
  New York City
305 7th Avenue, 12th Floor
New York, NY 10001
212-633-2930

Epilepsy Society of
  Southern New York, Inc.
One Blue Hill Plaza
PO Box 1745
Pearl River, NY 10965
914-627-0627
800-640-0371

Subunit:
Field Office, Orange County
200 Midway Park Drive
Middletown, NY 10920
914-344-0450

Epilepsy Association of the
  Capital District
Pine West Plaza
One United Way
Albany, NY 12205
518-456-7501
800-894-3223

North Carolina

Epilepsy Association of
  North Carolina, Inc.
3001 Spring Forest Rd.
Raleigh, NC 27604-2817
919-876-7788

Subunit:
Western Field Office
1401 East Seventh Street
Charlotte, NC 28204
704-377-EANC

North Dakota

Barnes, Cass, Cavilier,
  Grand Forks, Griggs, Nelson,
  Pembina, Ramsey, Ransom,
  Richland, Sargent, Steele, and
  Walsh Counties, ND are
  served by:
Epilepsy Foundation of
  Minnesota
777 Raymond Avenue
St. Paul, MN 55114

612-646-8675
800-779-0777

Ohio

Epilepsy Association of
  Central Ohio
115 West Main Street, Suite 300
Columbus, OH 43215
614-228-4401
800-878-3226

Subunit:
Licking County Branch
21 South First Street
Newark, OH 43055
614-345-1114

Epilepsy Council of Greater
  Cincinnati, Inc. (ECGC)
8 Centennial Plaza
895 Central Avenue
Cincinnati, OH 45202
513-721-2905

Subunit:
Warren County, OH (ECGC)
570 N. State, Rte. 741
Lebanon, OH 45036
513-925-2250

Subunit:
Epilepsy Association of
  Greater Louisville (EAGC)
334 East Broadway
Louisville, KY 40202
502-584-8817

Epilepsy Association of
  Western Ohio
803 East 5th Street, Suite C
Dayton, OH 45402
513-222-0127

Epilepsy Foundation of
  Northeast Ohio
2800 Euclid Avenue, Room 450
Cleveland, OH 44115
216-579-1330

Subunit:
EFNEO Lorain County Office
1875 North Ridge Road, Suite E
Lorain, OH 44055
216-277-6692

Epilepsy Center of
  Northwest Ohio
5405 Southwyck Blvd.
Toledo, OH 43614
419-867-5950
800-589-5958

Oregon

Epilepsy Association of Oregon
619 S.W. 11th Avenue, Suite 225
Portland, OR 97205
503-228-7651

Pennsylvania

Epilepsy Foundation of
  Southeastern Pennsylvania
128 Chestnut Street, Suite 104
Philadelphia, PA 19106
215-627-4442
800-887-7165

Epilepsy Foundation of
  Western Pennsylvania
Vocational Rehab Center
1323 Forbes Avenue, Suite 102
Pittsburgh, PA 15219
412-261-5880
800-361-5885

Subunit:
EFWP Epilepsy Resource Center
  of Central Pennsylvania
900 S. Arlington Ave., #236
Harrisburg, PA 17109
717-541-0301
800-336-0301

Puerto Rico

Soc Puertorriquena de Ayuda al
  Paciente con Epilepsia

Hospital Ruiz Soler
Calle Marginal Final
Bayamon, PR 00959
809-782-6200
809-782-6262

South Carolina

Epilepsy Association of the
  Midlands, Inc.
Logan Community School
815 Elmwood Avenue, Room 306
Columbia, SC 29201
803-733-6210

Tennessee

Epilepsy Foundation of
  West Tennessee
1750 Madison Avenue, Suite B-40
Memphis, TN 38104
901-272-3268

Subunit:
Field Office, EFWT
168 S. Forest Ave.
Camden, TN 38320
901-584-3906

Epilepsy Foundation of
  Greater Chattanooga
744 McCallie Avenue, Suite 421
Chattanooga, TN 37403
423-756-1771

Epilepsy Foundation of
  Greater Knoxville
PO Box #3156
Knoxville, TN 37927
423-522-4991
800-951-4991

Subunit:
Epilepsy Foundation of
  Northeast TN (EFGK)
207 N. Boone St., Suite 300
Johnson City, TN 37605
423-434-9196

Epilepsy Foundation of
  Middle Tennessee
2002 Richard Jones Rd., #C202
Nashville, TN 37215
615-269-7091
800-244-0768

Subunit:
EFMT, Parent Support Network
  and TAPS Program
319 Bethany Lane
Shelbyville, TN 37160
423-684-5222
800-697-3368

Texas

Dallas Epilepsy Association
2906 Swiss Avenue
Dallas, TX 75204
214-823-8809

Epilepsy Association of
  North Central Texas
2100 Circle Drive
Fort Worth, TX 76119
817-536-8693

Epilepsy Association of
  Houston/Gulf Coast
2650 Fountain View, Suite 316
Houston, TX 77507
713-789-6295

The Epilepsy Association of
  San Antonio/South Texas
5430 Fredericksburg Road, #508
San Antonio, TX 78229
210-308-9151

Utah

Epilepsy Association of Utah
641 E. 400 South
Salt Lake City, UT 84102
801-534-0210

Vermont

Epilepsy Association of Vermont
PO Box 6292
Rutland, VT 05702
802-775-1686
802-775-7675 (FAX)

Subunit:
Sulivan Hall
92 Ethan Allen Avenue
Colchester, VT 05446
802-655-4566

Virginia

Epilepsy Association of Virginia
The Highlands Center
Box BRH–UVA Health Sciences
  Center
Charlottesville, VA 22908
804-924-8678

Subunit:
Epilepsy Association of VA,
  Central Virginia Chapter
PO Box 15192
Richmond, VA 23227
804-257-7757

Alexandria, Arlington, Fairfax,
  Falls Church, Loudoun, and
  Prince William Counties, VA
  are served by the following
  affiliate:
Epilepsy Association for the
  National Capital Area
1331 H Street NW, Suite 1005
Washington, DC 20005
202-638-5229

Washington

Epilepsy Association of
  Washington
1306 Western Avenue, #308
Seattle, WA 98101
206-623-4366
800-752-3509

Clark County, WA is served by
the following affiliate:
Epilepsy Association of Oregon
619 S.W. 11th Avenue, Suite 225
Portland, OR 97205
503-228-7651

Wisconsin

Epilepsy Association of
Southeast Wisconsin
735 N. Water Street, Suite 701
Milwaukee, WI 53202
414-271-0110

Wisconsin Epilepsy Association
6400 Gisholt Drive, Suite 113
Madison, WI 53713
608-221-1210
800-733-1244

Subunit:
Epilepsy Education and Support
Group of the Racine/Kenosha
Area
5335 Chestnut Drive
Racine, WI 53402
414-639-3907

Subunit:
Epilepsy Education and Support
Group of the Manitowoc Area
832 Lincoln Boulevard
Manitowoc, WI 54220
414-683-3966

Epilepsy Center of
Western Wisconsin

513 S. Barstow Street
Eau Claire, WI 54701
715-834-4455
800-924-2105

Epilepsy Center South Central
7818 Big Sky Drive, Suite 117
Madison, WI 53719-4983
608-833-8888
800-657-4929

Midstate Epilepsy Association
1004 First Street, Suite 5
Stevens Point, WI 54481-2627
715-341-5811
800-924-9932

Subunit:
Outreach Office
903 2nd Street
Wausau, WI 54401-4705
715-845-2328

Epilepsy Association of
Southern Wisconsin, Inc.
201 South Water Street
Janesville, WI 53545
608-755-1821

Subunit:
Grant and Iowa Counties
PO Box 213
Lancaster, WI 53813
608-723-4488

Note: Douglas County is served
by the Epilepsy League of
Lake Superior, Inc.
(See Minnesota)

Appendix II

Related Books, Publications, and Videotapes

❖ ❖ ❖ ❖ ❖

❖ ❖ ❖ ❖ ❖

Children's Book Collection of the Epilepsy Foundation of America. To order, call 1-800-213-5821. Prices are current as of July 1, 1996 and are subject to change.

- Swanson, Susanne M. *My Friend Emily. A Story about Epilepsy and Friendship*. Writers Press Service, 1994, 35 pgs. Ages 5 to 10. Catalog #234MFE $5.99
- Dr. Wellbook Collection. *Dotty the Dalmatian has Epilepsy*. Tim Peters & Company, 1993, 16 pgs. Ages 2 to 6. Catalog #208DDB $4.95
- Moss, Deborah M. *Lee the Rabbit with Epilepsy*. Woodbine House, Inc., 1991, 23 pgs. Ages 3 to 6. Catalog #133LRB $12.95
- Buckel, Marian Carla and Buckel, Tiffany. *Mom, I Have a Staring Problem*. 1994, 24 pgs. Ages 6 to 10. Catalog #220MSP $3.95
- Pridmore, Saxby and McGrath, Mary. *Julia, Mungo, and the Earthquake*. Imagination Press, 1991, 47 pgs. Ages 6 to 12. Catalog #209QKE $7.95

Other Related Publications of the Epilepsy Foundation of America:
- *Seizure Man, First Aid for Seizures Comic,* Catalog #120MAN 86¢ EFA member; 95¢ nonmember
- *Because You Are My Friend,* Catalog #027BMF (English) 68¢ EFA member; 75¢ nonmember
- *Me and My World Storybook,* Catalog #015AAE $1.76 EFA member; $1.95 nonmember
- *Child's Guide to Seizure Disorders,* Catalog #078CGS 45¢ EFA member; 50¢ nonmember
- *Spiderman Battles the Myth Monster Comic,* Catalog #129SMM 68¢ EFA member; 75¢ nonmember

Videotapes of the Epilepsy Foundation of America:
- *I Have Epilepsy, Too,* Catalog #5101ET (English) $13.46 EFA member; $14.95 nonmember
- *Epilepsy In the Teen Years,* Catalog #515ETY $13.46 EFA member; $14.95 nonmember

Other books of interest:
- Devinsky, Orrin. *A Guide to Understanding and Living with Epilepsy.* F. A. Davis, 1994, 345 pgs. Ages 16 and up.
- Dodson, Edwin and Pellock, John M. (eds.). *Pediatric Epilepsy: Diagnosis and Therapy.* Demos 1993. Ages 16 and up.
- Dudley, Mark E. *Epilepsy.* Silver Burdett Press, 1997. Ages 10 and up.
- Gram, Lennart and Dam, Mogens. *Epilepsy Explained.* Munksgaard, Copenhagen, 1995, 208 pgs. Ages 16 and up.
- Gumnit, Robert J. *Your Child and Epilepsy: A Guide to Living Well.* Demos Vermande, 1995, 243 pgs. Ages 16 and up.
- Kaplan, Peter W., Loiseau, Pierre, Fisher, Robert S., and Jallon, Pierre. *Epilepsy A to Z.* Demos Vermande, 1995, 322 pgs. Ages 16 and up.
- Moshe, Solomon L., Pellock, John M., Salon, Matthew C. *The Parke-Davis Manual on Epilepsy. Useful Tips That Help You Get the Best Out of Life.* KSF Group, 1992. Ages 16 and up.
- Schachter, Steven C. *Brainstorms: Epilepsy in Our Words.* Raven Press, 1993, 104 pgs. Ages 16 and up.
- Schachter, Steven C. *The Brainstorms Companion: Epilepsy in Our View.* Raven Press, 1995, 134 pgs. Ages 16 and up.
- Wilner, Andrew N. *Epilepsy: 199 Answers (A Doctor Responds to His Patient's Questions).* Demos Vermande, 1996, 152 pgs. Ages 16 and up.

Appendix III

The Winning Kids Program

❖ ❖ ❖ ❖ ❖

❖ ❖ ❖ ❖ ❖

For a number of years, the Epilepsy Foundation of America (EFA) has conducted a national "Winning Kids" program. The program honors children with epilepsy who have overcome difficulties or succeeded in a special activity.

All EFA affiliates are invited to enter candidates in the program. Youngsters between 6 and 11 are eligible. The "Winning Kids" philosophy is a key part of the activity. Every one of the children entered by an affiliate is considered to be a Winning Kid. The program honors the achievements of children with epilepsy.

The Winning Kids subcommittee of the EFA then selects one of the Winning Kids to represent the nation's children with epilepsy for that year, beginning in November, which is National Epilepsy Month. These Winning Kids often participate in exciting activities such as visiting the White House, speaking at national conferences, and taking part in special fundraising events.

The following children who participated in the EFA Winning Kids program (first name is in parentheses) and their parents are represented in this book:

Mr. and Mrs. Patrick
  Carroll (Rebecca)
Fairport, NY

Ms. Carla Christo
  (Carla Simon)
Madison, WI

Ms. Vicki Edwards
  (Brittni)
Dallas, TX

Mr. and Mrs. Eric Flourie
  (Skyler)
Del Mar, CA

Mr. and Mrs. Ray Hurst
  (Douglas)
Houston, TX

Mr. and Mrs. Carl Jones
  (Lauren)
Bakersfield, CA

Mr. and Mrs. Douglas
  Lewis (Jeffrey)
Esopus, NY

Ms. Bernardita McGilvery
  (Christopher)
Honolulu, HI

Mr. and Mrs. Larry
    Mcpherson (Robert)
Millington, MI

Mr. and Mrs. Stephen
    Schisel (Luke)
Boise, ID

Mr. and Mrs. Peter
    Schneider (Russell)
Rice Lake, WI

Mr. William Shine (Katey)
St. Joseph, MI

Mr. and Mrs. Robert
    Sweeney (Sarah)
Niskayuna, NY

Mr. and Mrs. Mark Wiese
    (Aaron)
Silverdale, WA

Information about the Artwork

On June 24, 1995, an event was held in New York City during which 11 prominent artists were willingly upstaged by a group of young amateurs. These youngsters who drew, painted, photographed, and created works of art all had something in common. They each had epilepsy and used the occasion to reflect their feelings about the effect of the condition on each of their lives.

The FACES (Fight Against Childhood Epilepsy and Seizures) Art Day was sponsored by the New York University-Hospital for Joint Diseases Comprehensive Epilepsy Center and the New York University Art Department. The event was developed and coordinated by Janis E. Svendsen, mother of a child with refractory seizures, and a FACES Steering Committee member. Its purpose was to provide support for a new center for children with epilepsy. Selected works were auctioned off at Sotheby's.

The artwork was created under the guidance of Paul Bloodgood, Sarah Charlesworth, Sandi Fellman, Molissa Fenley, Paula Hayes, Jules Heller, Leonard Lehrer, Kristin Oppenheim, Richard Prince, Collier Schorr, and Meyer Vaisman. Four pieces of art from that show appear in the center of this book.

Index

❖ ❖ ❖ ❖ ❖

The numbers refer to the selection number found at the beginning of each passage.

FEELINGS OF THE CHILD

Acceptance, 14
Activities limited, 12, 14, 50, 52
Angry, 36, 45
Belief in God, 4
Denial, 45
Depression, 6, 8, 15, 30, 43
Embarrassment, 4, 23, 43, 46
Fear of dying, 15, 34
Friends are afraid, 14, 50
Friends are helpful, 6, 29, 30, 32, 39, 40, 43
Frightened, 6, 18, 24, 30, 34, 40, 46
Frustrated, 10, 18, 24
Hard to tell friends, 2, 50
Hope that seizures will stop, 1, 41, 43, 50
Jealousy, 23
Live normal life, 11, 15, 29, 48, 52, 53
Medication side effects, 6, 20, 50, 52, 53
Memory difficulties, 6
Need to educate others, 36
Others make fun of child, 4, 19, 20, 24, 34, 36, 39
Upset about driving, 6, 15, 50

Urge to laugh, 6
Wish to stop having blood tests, 1, 16
Wish to stop seeing doctors, 1
Wish to stop taking medication, 1, 12, 21, 43
Worry about future, 12, 16

FEELINGS OF THE PARENTS

Acceptance, 20, 42, 44, 51
Anger, 13
Appreciate life, 8, 28, 32, 51
Behavior problems, 11, 32, 36, 45, 46, 49
Belief in God, 13, 51
Belief that person with seizures is kidding around, 6, 18, 48
Concern about other children, 17, 22, 49
Confidence, 17, 37
Denial, 1, 49
Depression, 19
Devastated, 37
Discipline issues, 11, 49
Disappointment, 3, 7
Encourage child, 2
Fear about brain tumor, 1, 15, 43

SEIZURE OBSERVATIONS BY THE CHILD

SEIZURE OBSERVATIONS BY THE PARENTS